W9-AJP-328

surrendering hunger

surrendering hunger

365 DEVOTIONS FOR WHOLENESS

REVISED, 15ᵀᴴ ANNIVERSARY EDITION

Jan Johnson

PARACLETE PRESS
BREWSTER, MASSACHUSETTS

3D

Surrendering Hunger : 365 Devotions for Wholeness

2008 First Printing this edition

Copyright © 1993, 2008 by Jan Johnson

ISBN: 978-1-55725-636-2

Unless otherwise noted, all Scripture quotations are from the Holy
Bible, New International Version. Copyright © 1973, 1978, 1984
International Bible Society. Used by permission of Zondervan Bible
Publishers.

Original edition catalogued with the Library of Congress as follows:
Library of Congress Cataloging-in-Publication Data
Johnson, Jan.
    Surrendering hunger: 365 devotions for Christians recovering from
    eating disorders / Jan Johnson. — 1st ed. p. cm.
    Includes index.
    ISBN 0-06-064251-3
    1. Eating disorders—Patients—Prayer-book and devotions—English.
    2. Devotional calendars. I. Title.
    BV491035J64   1993   92-54535
    242'.4—dc20   CIP

10 9 8 7 6 5 4 3 2 1

All rights reserved. No part of this book may be reproduced, stored
in an electronic retrieval system, or transmitted in any form or by
any means—electronic, mechanical, photocopy, recording, or any
other—except for brief quotations in printed reviews, without the prior
permission of the publisher.

Published by Paraclete Press
Brewster, Massachusetts
www.paracletepress.com
Printed in the United States of America

Introduction

Those of us struggling with food issues, compulsive eating, or compulsive dieting, know that working through these things is not a quick process. It doesn't happen in a week or a month or even a year. It doesn't happen after a visit to a dietician or going to weekly support group meetings. We work on these issues every day, several times a day. We are on a journey.

The meditations in this book are designed to add strength and hope to the daily journey. I have based them on verses found throughout the Bible because my own walk has awakened me spiritually to God as the loving parent presented there.

If you're a little fuzzy on the spiritual-growth terms used, the glossary defines some of those, too. If perhaps you once had faith in God but now you're not sure, this book allows you to take a second look at faith and the nature of God's character.

I have used the masculine pronouns *he, him,* and *his* throughout this book to refer to God because adequate pronouns do not exist. The Bible says that God's image is both male and female (Genesis 1:27), so I believe that God's personhood is also both male and female. I regret limiting God by using only masculine pronouns, but I trust that "he" understands and I hope you do, too.

Day 1 Do I Trust God?

READ | Genesis 2:16–17

And the LORD God commanded the man, "You are free to eat from any tree in the garden; but you must not eat from the tree of the knowledge of good and evil, for when you eat of it you will surely die."

From the beginning, eating has been a problem for humans. But in the garden and even now the problem is much deeper. I'm not sure whom I trust and don't trust. My impression of God is so distorted that I don't trust God easily. Can I trust God to love me as I am, to value me in spite of my failures?

I have allowed other powers in this world to tell me what God is like. Teachers and friends valued outward actions instead of inward motivations; parents, being only human, did not portray the unconditional love of God. I need to know God better and find out what he's really like. As I do this, I can put my trust in God who, most of all, deserves my trust.

Thank you, God, for helping me to put my trust in you
and brush away all those other images of you.

REFLECT | *The core issue in my life is not my eating problem but my lack of trust in God.*

Day 2 I Didn't Do It!

READ | Genesis 3:12–13

The man said, "The woman you put here with me—she gave me some fruit from the tree, and I ate it."... The woman said, "The serpent deceived me, and I ate."

I have been like the man in this passage—putting the blame on someone else. I can take responsibility for my compulsive overeating, my short temper, and my laziness.

I see the destructive results of blaming others:

- blaming others distracts me from examining my own defects of character;
- blaming the same people over and over makes me dislike them more;
- blaming others keeps my life in an uproar; it robs me of any serenity I have.

For my own good, I stop blaming and start admitting when I'm wrong.

God, help me recognize when I blame others,
and help me admit my own fault in the matter.

REFLECT | *Time spent blaming is time wasted.*

Day 3 Releasing the Anger

READ | Genesis 4:6–7

Then the LORD said to Cain, "Why are you angry? Why is your face downcast? . . . [sin] desires to have you, but you must master it."

I'm like Cain when I'm angry. I try to bury my anger and put on a happy face. But like Cain's, my face is downcast, and I can't seem to shake my anger unless I work through it. But that is too difficult, so I secretly numb my anger by overeating or starving. Then I can put the happy face back on for a while, although I never know when my anger will leak.

God intervened to help Cain deal with his anger. I often feel the same nudge from God myself. I'm learning that when this happens I can work through my anger in ways that don't hurt anyone else. I talk it out with a friend or at a support group, I journal about it, or I take one of my rather loud prayer walks. Then I've released it, and I'm free of my anger and my need to overeat or deny myself excessively.

Thank you for prompting me
to surrender my anger to you.

REFLECT | *To admit and then let go of anger is to find life, one day at a time.*

✓Day 4 How Much Is Enough?

READ | Psalm 104:27–28
These all look to you to give them their food at the proper time. . . . When you open your hand, they are satisfied with good things.

As I start my day, I ask God to show me how much food is enough to sustain me properly. When I sit down at the table, that amount may seem like too little or too much, but I can trust that God is opening his hand to me. I trust that this amount will satisfy me physically even if it doesn't satisfy my emotional needs. I will now have other ways to satisfy my emotional needs: relationships, journaling, and prayer.

I, who have not trusted others well, am taking a big step by committing my food to God. This toughens and strengthens my relationship with him as I ask, "Are you sure about this, God?" Then I walk in that trust.

My daily food is a sacred gift from you,
and I value your judgments.

REFLECT | *I can trust God, the blesser himself, to distribute his blessings well.*

Day 5 Getting Beyond Myself

READ | Genesis 12:3

. . . and all peoples on earth will be blessed through you.

Am I working on this area of my life just so I can look good and impress others? Is my goal to have a nice life and not be a pain in the neck to anyone? Do I exist only to look within myself all day?

Yes, I need to look within myself, but also beyond myself. I see that God put me on earth to benefit other people. I tried to help others in the past, but my obsession with food handicaps me. I thought more about satisfying my neediness than about how I could serve others. My prayers were filled with pleas to relieve my own problems rather than inquiries about how I could follow God's will in every aspect of my life.

As I surrender to God, I rediscover God's purposes for my life because he teaches me how to get my needs met in healthy ways. I'm free to truly care about other people.

God, help me see that I am distracted by
my weight problems instead of being challenged
to serve you with my whole life.

REFLECT | *Self-improvement is never a big enough reason to change; fulfilling God's purposes is.*

Day 6 Shortcuts Can Get Me Lost

READ | Genesis 21:10

Get rid of that slave woman and her son, for that slave woman's son will never share in the inheritance with my son Isaac.

4

I want to feel better and look better, but I don't want to give up my own desires regarding food. Isn't there a shortcut?, I wonder.

Abraham tried to take a shortcut to God's will by having a son, Ishmael, with a slave woman. When Ishmael made life miserable for Abraham's later son, Isaac (the son God intended Abraham to have), Ishmael had to leave.

My eating problem is my Ishmael. It is my scheme to manage pain, feel better, and perform well in the chaos of me. But it is an unhealthy way to live, and I have to get rid of it.

Even though I may take the long way around to maintain a proper weight, I benefit so much from finding healthy ways to relate to God, others, and myself. I find my Isaac, God's true path for me.

Once again, I give my compulsions to you and
ask for healthier ways to deal with life.

REFLECT | *I surrender my destructive shortcuts to God.*

Day 7 I surrender my destructive shortcuts to God

READ | Genesis 21:17, 19
Do not be afraid; God has heard the boy crying as he lies there. . . . Then God opened [Hagar's] eyes and she saw a well of water.

Will God help me get out of this mess I've made? No, I don't deserve it.

But God helps those who mess up, too. Hagar was grieving and dying of thirst in the desert because she had made the worst of a bad situation. But God provided a well for her and her son. Even though she was more than partly at fault, he put the well there for her.

I am like Hagar. I am more than partly at fault for my being overweight (or underweight). I have isolated myself; I have tried to work it out on my own; I have misled others about my problem. Even though I am guilty of these things, God is still there for me. I don't have to be one hundred percent innocent for God to rescue me.

God, I am grateful that you take care of me
and meet my needs even when I mess up.

REFLECT | *God loves because he's faithful, not because I'm innocent.*

Day 8 A Promise in Stone

READ | Genesis 31:52
This heap [of stones] is a witness, and this pillar is a witness, that I will not go past this heap to your side to harm you. . . .

Are promises made to be broken? I have broken so many promises to myself to diet or to eat properly or to exercise more. I know the pain of broken promises.

One recovering manipulator, Jacob, and his enemy, Laban, set up a pile of stones to cement their promise not to harm each other. My friends who are struggling with food issues (some of whom may be in my support group) become witnesses of what I commit myself to do and not do. I promise them that I will make an effort to eat sensibly and make healthy choices. I promise to pray for everyone in the group every day. I promise to start exercising. Their simple presence in my life, like the pile of stones, reminds me of my promise in a concrete way. If I fail, I have these human witnesses to forgive me and help me start over.

> Please give me the strength to use
> the powerful tool of accountability.

REFLECT | *Accountability is teamwork, and it puts more strength on my side.*

Day 9 Regret Reduction
READ | Genesis 32:24—25, 31

So Jacob was left alone, and a man wrestled with him till daybreak. When the man saw that he could not overpower him, he touched the socket of Jacob's hip so that his hip was wrenched. . . . [Jacob] was limping because of his hip.

Like others who have trafficked in eating issues, I have done a miserable disservice to my body. Like Jacob, I am limping. My metabolism is slowed so that weight doesn't come off or stay off easily. My junk-food eating has sped along my hypoglycemia. These *limps* aren't endearing to me, but I don't regret them, either. They are memorials to the great battle I am fighting. They hint at how much more damaged I could be if I don't continue to surrender food to God.

My battle wounds are signs that I am a seasoned person who has acquired wisdom the hard way. I have struggled with God, with others, with food, and with a culture that worships food and thinness. I have overcome because I have surrendered to God my valiant attempts to win the wrestling match with food.

God, help me see my wounds as reminders
of how far I've come.

REFLECT | *I can live with the negative physical effects
of my past eating habits and not resent them or beat myself up over
them. Tomorrow is a new day.*

Day 10 Becoming Willing to Forgive

READ | Genesis 50:20
*You intended to harm me, but God intended it for good to accomplish
what is now being done. . . .*

Surrender involves forgiving those who have intentionally
harmed me. At first I may forgive because it's the smart thing
to do. I know that if I hold grudges, I will overeat or starve to
relieve the bad feelings my grudges produce.

As I progress in surrendering my life to God, I see why I'm
so unwilling to forgive others: I don't trust God to keep me
from further harm. In today's verse, Joseph trusted God and
forgave his brothers because he could see how God's plan had
worked to benefit everyone. Even if I can't see a master plan,
I can trust the Master to reroute someone else's devious plan to
my advantage. I surrender my bitterness, not because I trust
the person I forgive, but because I trust God.

Help me face my grudges and bitterness and
turn them over to you, God.

REFLECT | *Today I trust God with my bitterness.*

Day 11　Fullness Issues

READ　|　Joel 2:26

You will have plenty to eat, until you are full, and you will praise the name of the LORD your God, who has worked wonders for you; never again will my people be shamed.

Can I trust God to make my stomach feel good again—to give me a sense of fullness or to relieve it? If I order a salad for lunch, will I survive? If I scoop a proper amount of food onto my plate, will it satisfy me? Will it be too little or too much?

Eating sensibly means following a reasonable eating plan and surrendering these emotional eating issues to God. I must trust him to help me eat an appropriate amount and feel good about it. I must not panic and grab more or put some back.

If I try to eat normally, God will provide exactly what I need emotionally.

Help me feel full but not stuffed
with the right amounts of food.

REFLECT　|　*A sensible eating plan provides enough.*

Day 12　When Their Faults Are My Faults

READ　|　Exodus 2:12–13

[Moses] killed the Egyptian and hid him. . . . The next day he . . . asked the one in the wrong, "Why are you hitting your fellow Hebrew?"

When I get upset with people, I'm often guilty of the same things they do. I don't like judgmental people, but I judge quickly. I don't like grumpy people, but I can be grumpy. When I haven't worked out a problem in my own life, I spot it easily in others' lives—much like Moses who tried to break up a fight the day after he had murdered someone!

To truly surrender my whole life I have to quit taking inventories of other people's faults. I take responsibility for my own faults instead. I ask God to show me what I need to do to grow spiritually.

The only person I should try to change is myself, so I can get on with life and let God take care of others.

God, show me my character defects and
help me release them to you.

REFLECT | *I will be able to help others more when I have faced my own faults.*

Day 13 Scared to Step Out

READ | Exodus 4:13
But Moses said, "O Lord, please send someone else to do it!"

It's scary to pay attention to the promptings of God, and it's scary to ignore them. My love for my eating behaviors tells me to ignore God's promptings because they get in the way of my getting what I feel I need most—food.

As God's peace quiets the thunder of my compulsion, God's promptings seem louder. Sometimes I feel as if I'm standing in front of a burning bush, saying, "God, please ask someone else to start a support group . . . or to volunteer at the street mission."

As I face my fear and wait and pray, God plants a desire within me that is stronger than the fear. So I take the plunge. When I follow God's prompting (not my own grandiose desire for applause), it's more rewarding than I could have imagined.

God, help me listen to your promptings and follow them.

R E F L E C T | *To follow God's promptings is to enjoy the little excitements of life.*

Day 14 Look, I Don't Understand

R E A D | Exodus 12:22
Take a bunch of hyssop, dip it into the blood in the basin and put some of the blood on the top and on both sides of the door frame.

If I had been an Israelite hearing the instructions in today's verse, I would have said, "Forget it. That's a disgusting idea." Of course, I've thought that attending support groups and calling others for help was ridiculous, too. When I'm eating too much, few helpful ideas make sense to me.

Yet I see what the Israelites could not see—that the blood above and to the sides of the door frame form the three upper points of the cross of Christ. In a sense, the Israelites were calling on the power of Christ by putting blood on their door frames. And as I practice eating better, and I attend my support group, and I make telephone calls, I'm turning over my hunger and my need to control to Christ. I need his power to help me.

Help me to use the proven tools of
support groups, telephone calls, and prayer to
surrender to you even though their
importance eludes me.

R E F L E C T | *To do is to understand.*

Day 15 Choosing for Myself

R E A D | Daniel 1:8
But Daniel resolved not to defile himself with the royal food and wine. . . .

Daniel, a spiritual person (he was later arrested for praying three times a day), determined that his eating pattern would include vegetables and water. Even though this was inconvenient, he found a way to follow it.

Choosing my own healthy eating plan is full of possibilities for rationalizations, but it is still my choice. With God's help, I can choose wise habits that temper my drivenness. In time, he leads me to refine and change my eating patterns as I need to. I trust him to show me what to do and to help me see when I'm kidding myself.

God, you know my eating behaviors better than anyone else. Please show me the best eating plan.

R E F L E C T | *Choosing my own eating plan is a risky but wise step in my growth.*

Day 16 Choosing Foods Wisely

R E A D | Daniel 1:15–16
At the end of ten days they looked healthier and better nourished than any of the young men who ate the royal food. So the guard took away their choice food and the wine they were to drink and gave them vegetables instead.

As I practice eating sensibly, mealtime is no longer the highlight of my day. I don't need my favorite foods to satisfy me, because food is no longer a reward. I want to eat nutritious food for lunch so I can be more alert afterward.

It is a miracle that alertness is becoming more important than my appetite! I remember days when nothing was more important than appetite. There is hope for me yet!

Thank you, God, for the gift of food, and
help me use it to help my body function well.

REFLECT | *I eat simply to nourish my body—imagine that!*

Day 17 Serenity in Stillness

READ | Exodus 14:14
The LORD will fight for you; you need only be still.

If I am going to stop overeating or undereating, I have to stop panicking, too. As a compulsive controller, I move into the panic mode when a crisis strikes.

No more. Now I take care of what is within my control, knowing that most things in life are not within my control. Often I'm trapped like the Israelites were between a powerful Egyptian army and the Red Sea. I am learning to trust that God is going to part that Red Sea—without my interference.

When I am confident that God will intervene, I have serenity. Others may urge me to panic, to plot, and to coerce, but I "need only be still." Finally, I am learning to watch and wait for God to part the Red Seas in my life.

Thank you, God, that you invade impossible situations
and give me the serenity I need.

REFLECT | *To wait and be still is an unexplainable serenity.*

Day 18 God's Learning Curve

READ | Exodus 15:2
The Lord is my strength and my song; he has become my salvation.

I thought I knew God. Yet as I work on food issues in my life I find my need to lean on God as never before. He becomes my strength.

I also thank God for my progress, even though it is slow. I celebrate with him in prayer and in the way I report to my struggling friends. He becomes my song.

As I examine my character defects and allow God to permeate every area of my life, no matter how disgusting, I become identified with him and begin to have a sense of oneness with him. He's becoming my daily salvation in everything I do.

God, please come into my life in a greater way.

REFLECT | *Leaning on God is how it begins; oneness with him is how it continues.*

Day 19 Becoming Whole

READ | Exodus 16:14–15
Thin flakes like frost on the ground appeared on the desert floor. When the Israelites saw it, they said to each other, "What is it?"

I look at the food on my plate as if it were manna and say, "What is it?" The sight of five ounces of broccoli is a strange sight. Have I traded in chocolate binges for this? It isn't much of a prize.

This is reality. I have turned my back on the power of food. It can no longer be a soothing friend or a weapon for control. It is only a nourishing substance.

If I were on a diet, this healthy food might make me grouchy, but true healing from food obsession is different. I fill my life with prayer, meditation, reading, and serving others. I am finally involved in worthwhile activities that do not involve overconsuming or underconsuming food!

God, help me shift my focus from food to life.

REFLECT | *I used to live to eat; now I eat to live.*

Day 20 Meeting with God

READ | Exodus 19:17
Then Moses led the people out of the camp to meet with God, and they stood at the foot of the mountain.

At regular intervals, I meet with God. Yes, it's difficult to go "out of the camp" of my daily life for a few minutes or hours, but it's so rewarding when I do.

I don't expect fireworks or great revelations from my time with God. I expect only to meet God in some way, and because he's such a varied being, I meet him in various ways. I hear him talk through the Scripture, through my meditation on it, through my own journaling and prayers, and through the stillness of being with him.

I come away knowing that I am loved by God, knowing that I am no longer useless because he has great designs for me.

Thank you for meeting with me, God,
and letting me know that I am loved.

REFLECT | *Meeting with God becomes something I look forward to.*

Day 21 Can Good Come Out of Anger?

READ | Exodus 32:19
When Moses approached the camp and saw the calf and the dancing, his anger burned and he threw the tablets out of his hands, breaking them to pieces. . . .

Anger is like fire. It can be used for good purposes when it motivates us to right wrongs. But too often I express my righteous anger in unhealthy ways. Like Moses, I may have good reasons to be angry, but I hurt the people I love the most.

If I'm to surrender these behaviors, I have to look at my anger and make choices about it. When people and situations frustrate me, I can allow the passion stirred within me to motivate me to do something constructive instead of destructive. I can calm myself and say or do something helpful. My anger can do some good, as fire warms a cold world.

Take my anger, Lord, and use it in a positive way.

REFLECT | *When I give my anger to God, great things happen.*

Day 22 Being Versus Doing

READ | Exodus 33:14
The LORD replied, "My Presence will go with you, and I will give you rest."

In the past, I thought God wanted me to be up and doing every minute. I frantically tried to figure out how to please him, and I did and did and did.

I've come to see that God loves me and sees me as something more than a machine. Not only does he encourage me to rest, but also he gives me rest. As I acknowledge his continuous presence in my life, I can abide in his rest and taste some of that serenity I've been chasing. I refuel so that in the fray of battle, I am more reassured and less panicked.

> Thank you, God, for helping me learn to rest
> in your presence.

REFLECT | *God wants me to "be" with him; he will lead me to the proper amount of doing.*

Day 23 Moving Beyond Failures

READ | Exodus 34:1
The LORD said to Moses, "Chisel out two stone tablets like the first ones, and I will write on them the words that were on the first tablets, which you broke."

When I make mistakes, no one judges me more harshly than I judge myself. To me, mistakes aren't something I can correct, but catastrophes I must regret for the rest of my life. That's one reason I feel such a need to overeat and to control my overeating.

I marvel at how God forgave Moses for breaking the stones on which the Ten Commandments were written and simply told him to write them again. I want to be that kind of parent to myself and to my children. When I fall flat on my face, I want to get up, brush myself off, and say, "Let's try again."

Even if I fail today, especially in the food area, I want to forgive myself and say, "God is helping me begin again."

> Thank you, God, for picking up the pieces of myself
> and letting me start over.

Failure doesn't have to defeat me unless I beat myself up over it.

Day 24 Others May, I Choose Not To

READ | Leviticus 18:3
You must not do as they do in Egypt, where you used to live, and you must not do as they do in the land of Canaan, where I am bringing you. Do not follow their practices.

It feels as if everyone around me is stuffing themselves on sugary foods or talking about losing weight and skipping meals. They don't seem to have any problems. Couldn't I just this once do the same thing?

I know what I need to do: adopt a sane, healthy eating plan in my life and to grow in the light God has given me. It doesn't matter if my culture is food-oriented or my friends overeat or diet incessantly. I now know I am important to God and to others in my support group. I will not overeat, under-eat, or overspend, even though my culture says this extreme behavior is normal.

Help me, God, to know and love you so well that your
voice blocks out the voices of excess in my culture.

REFLECT | *Others may follow my culture, but I choose not to do so.*

Day 25 Progress I Don't Understand

READ | Leviticus 26:8
Five of you will chase a hundred, and a hundred of you will chase ten thousand, and your enemies will fall by the sword before you.

As difficult as dealing with an eating problem can be, there are small improvements that I can't explain.

I struggle so long with chocolate and turn down one candy bar and suddenly all kinds of food have less appeal for me. I focus on quieting my voice with my children and it seems hopeless, but then I find I'm less frustrated with my co-workers. I progress when I'm not looking, and I can't explain why.

That's the beauty of it. With God, five soldiers can defeat one hundred soldiers. If I could explain it, I would claim I won in my strength and feel proud, then I would fall. This way, I can only report my progress to my friends and celebrate with them. These small moments of grace become inside jokes with God.

Work in me, using your mysterious paths, God,
and I promise to cooperate.

REFLECT | *God's ways are mysterious, and that's OK.*

Day 26 My Conscience, My Friend

READ | Numbers 5:6–7

When a man or woman wrongs another . . . that person is guilty and must confess the sin he has committed. He must make full restitution for his wrong. . . .

When I have a guilty conscience, I try to ignore it but I still feel needy inside. Neediness stirs up my drivenness, and I want to overeat or punish myself by undereating.

If I'm to abstain from these behaviors, I have to confess my faults, ask forgiveness, and make amends. It isn't pleasant to face people and situations I would rather forget, but it cleanses me. I'm able to live with myself without the numbing effect of food.

Asking forgiveness and making amends sets a pattern of taking responsibility for my hurtful actions. The next time I think about doing something hurtful, my conscience awakens and pleads with me, "Please don't make me confess and make restitution again! Anything but that!" So I change my path and do what seems to be the kindest, most helpful thing.

God, please give me the courage to confess my mistakes and make amends.

REFLECT | *A clean conscience decreases my need for food.*

Day 27 When Griping Grips Me

READ | Numbers 11:1

Now the people complained about their hardships in the hearing of the LORD, and when he heard them his anger was aroused.

Griping is often a well-developed hobby for those of us who are excessive. Take me anywhere and I can come up with five things that are wrong with any person, place, or thing. The more I gripe, the more I feel the need to manage and control.

So griping becomes one more thing I confess to my support group. I can try a simple accountability such as not complaining for twenty-four hours. The next night and next day I catch myself with my mouth open, ready to spew forth cranky complaints, but nothing comes out. When people say, "What were you going to say?" I can smile.

Changing my behavior this way is difficult but wonderful. Life is so much better. I do this as often as I need to until I find that I feel more grateful all the time.

Thank you, Lord, that while you help me
process my thoughts and feelings you also
help me break destructive habits.

REFLECT | *My hopelessness fades as my complaining fades.*

✓Day 28 Better Off Where?

READ | Numbers 11:18
*The LORD heard you when you wailed, "If only we had meat to eat! We
were better off in Egypt!"*

When I long to return to satisfying myself with food, I
don't know what I'm asking for. I resemble the Israelites who
became tired of eating manna every day. Their appetites were
so distorted that they said they were better off in Egypt as slaves
making bricks, because sometimes they got meat to eat.

I have the same choice. I can choose slavery or freedom.
On the days when eating drives me, much of my life is clouded
by my appetite. I choose social activities based on whether
or not food is served; I choose friends who also overeat or
undereat; I make the rounds of convenience stores for junk
food. Now I'm free to choose jobs, friendships, and social
activities with no thought of how close they take me to an ice
cream parlor.

God, show me just how much my eating enslaves me.

REFLECT | *I'm better off without the enslavement of un-
healthy eating.*

Day 29   What Humility Isn't

R E A D | Numbers 12:3
Now Moses was a very humble man, more humble than anyone else on the face of the earth.

Humility is important in surrendering. But what does humility mean?

Does it mean I can't make decisions? No, Moses decided (with God's direction) to lead a nation out of slavery.

Does it mean I never feel anger? No, Moses was rightfully angry when the Israelites worshiped a golden calf.

Does it mean I'm always afraid—or never afraid? Neither. Moses was reluctant to lead the Israelites, but he did it after he was convinced that God would supply the power.

Humility means that I let God be in charge of public relations. I don't have to impress anyone or compare myself to anyone to feel better about myself. I can be me and let God take care of the rest.

God, I give you my worries about how I look
and who likes me.

R E F L E C T | *Humility means self-forgetfulness instead of self-obsession.*

Day 30   Trusting As I Go

R E A D | Numbers 13:31
But the men who had gone up with him said, "We can't attack those people; they are stronger than we are."

My eating has been my comfort zone. The thought of eating sensibly sometimes seems too scary to pursue. Like the men in today's verse who were afraid to take possession of their promised land, I claim, "I can't attack my eating habits. They are stronger than I am."

But that is not true. These men were afraid and exaggerated the obstacles. So do I.

I need only a small amount of trust—only enough to step out and go to a support group. As I move along, my trust in God grows to fit the increasing risks—taking an inventory, making amends, and becoming whole.

Each risk stretches me enough to take the next step.

God, please help me let go of my insatiable need for safety
and cling to your protection.

REFLECT | *Only by going out on a limb can I get to the fruit.*

Day 31 God Defends Me

READ | Numbers 14:10
But the whole assembly talked about stoning them. Then the glory of the LORD appeared at the Tent of Meeting to all the Israelites.

What do I do when people stone me with words even though I am innocent? Moses and Aaron did nothing and waited for God to display his presence and power. I am learning that there's a difference between honest seekers who want to understand me and quick condemners who want to blame me. Some criticism is helpful; some is not.

If the criticism isn't helpful, it's useless to defend myself. Offering a calm, logical defense does not diffuse the anger of my accusers. In fact, it often inflames it further.

As I improve my conscious contact with God, I try to follow his guidance concerning the times I should defend myself and the times I should be silent and let God defend me.

Please, God, give me the serenity to avoid making exhausting defenses when it will do no good.

REFLECT | *God rules, and the truth will be revealed at the appropriate time.*

Day 32 God's Balanced Character

READ | Numbers 14:18

The LORD is slow to anger, abounding in love and forgiving sin and rebellion. Yet he does not leave the guilty unpunished.

Many people see God as:
- all justice: a punishing tyrant
- all mercy: a permissive, pushover parent.

The idea that God can be just and merciful at the same time is paradoxical, but real. I understand this only as I practice it. God can work in my life when I admit I have a food problem and make amends (justice), but also when I forgive myself (mercy).

This balance of justice and mercy spreads through my life as I'm more eager to be fair yet forgiving when I clear up misunderstandings with a friend. Those days of harshness one day and permissiveness the next are fading, and I'm finding the balance I've needed for a long time.

Thank you, God, for being just and merciful,
fair yet forgiving.

√Day 33 Presenting My Anger to God

READ | Numbers 16:15

Then Moses became very angry and said to the LORD, "Do not accept their offering. I have not . . . wronged any of them!"

Can I hide my anger from God? I sure try. Sometimes I try so hard to hide it from others, too, that I end up unleashing it when I least expect it.

Like Moses, though, I can take my anger to God. I can lay out the problem before him. In this process, I sometimes discover that I am at fault, and then I go to the person I offended and make amends. At other times, I am angry for a good reason, as Moses was.

By presenting my anger to God, I am taking it to the only one who can do anything about it. God can calm me. He can also correct or change my opponent in ways I can't. With God's help, I can release the anger.

God, thank you for loving me when
I'm angry, accepting my anger, and helping
me resolve it.

REFLECT | *I trust God enough to show him my hurts instead of hiding them from him.*

Day 34 Blaming God

READ | Numbers 21:5
They spoke against God and against Moses, and said, "Why have you brought us up out of Egypt to die in the desert?"

As my weight problem continued I felt hopeless. Nothing worked, and I developed a bitterness toward God. In my most frustrated moments, I prayed, "Why aren't you helping me, God?" I blamed God because I was on the wrong path.

Now that I'm surrendering this problem to God, I recognize my tendency to blame him for things. My problem is similar to the Israelites' problem. I am on the right path, but it's longer and harder than I thought it would be. It's easy to accuse God of deceiving me and breaking his promises.

So when I start accusing, I stop. I ask myself if I'm creating this problem through my own unhealthy behavior. Or am I growing impatient with myself, even though God is patient with me?

God, I admit my bitterness toward you and
ask for your forgiveness and healing.

REFLECT | *Bitterness hardens my heart; surrender nourishes hope.*

Day 35 I Have Enough

READ | Deuteronomy 5:21
You shall not set your desire on your neighbor's house or land . . . his ox or donkey, or anything that belongs to your neighbor.

I used to think everyone else had it better. One friend had a better marriage, another had a better car, and they all had a better life. When I think this way, I'm saying that God doesn't know what he's doing, that he hasn't given me what I need to make it in life, and that what he provides for me will never be enough, or at least good enough.

Gratefulness changes my attitude. I can be grateful for God's unconditional love and that he chooses to delight in me. No matter what I weigh, no matter how I look, I can be grateful that he has given me everything I need to survive and to grow in wholeness. I can even be grateful for people I know who have acquired more than I have.

> God, I am grateful that you have supplied
> exactly what I need for today.

REFLECT | *God, I am grateful that you have supplied exactly what I need for today.*

Day 36 Good, Better, or Best?

READ | Deuteronomy 6:5
Love the LORD your God with all your heart and with all your soul and with all your strength.

There are so many *good* things to seek. I can seek happiness, I can seek health, I can seek a good marriage, but these things will never be enough to fill the empty space inside me. Seeking God and loving him with everything I've got is the only thing that will be enough.

Yet I still find myself focusing on the extras. When I weigh the right amount, I'll be able to wear more of my clothes.

Without that distraction of food, I'll be able to perform better on my job than ever before. With all the patience I'm learning, I'll be the best co-worker I've ever been.

All those things are good, but they aren't the very best. And they are never reason enough to change the direction of my life or even more specifically to change my way of eating. The best reason to surrender this problem is to know God better and find his direction for my life.

> God, help me move beyond good motives
> and to want more than anything to seek more of you
> and your purpose for my life.

REFLECT | *To seek God is to find life.*

Day 37 Will My Progress Continue?

READ | Deuteronomy 6:10–12

When the LORD your God brings you into the land . . . be careful that you do not forget the LORD, who brought you out of Egypt, out of the land of slavery.

Success doesn't have to be a spoiler. With whatever progress I experience I have a choice. I can use that progress to move on, or I can use it to slide, thinking that I've done something about my problem and can now coast.

On the other hand, I bring my progress before God, my family, and my support group, and we celebrate it together. I can get the affirmation I need. I can avoid that rebellious part of me that runs ahead of myself and ruins things, and then snickers, *What made you think things would ever go well for you?*

It's time to lay down those old attitudes of laziness and spoiling. I can take up serenity and peace.

> Thank you, God, for my progress,
> however small it may be, and help me hang
> on to it when I get discouraged.

REFLECT | *Affirmation can spur me on.*

Day 38 Compromising

READ | Deuteronomy 7:2b
Make no treaty with them, and show them no mercy.

Sure, I said that I would eat three meals a day, but I can't sleep without a bedtime snack. Or I devour chips and dip and call it a meal. Or I sense that God is working overtime by the way the fast-food drive-through lines are so long and the convenience store is out of my favorite junk food. But then I make a treaty with the enemy and drive miles out of my way to get the food I crave. I don't trust God's power to get me through my neediness.

One of the deceits of eating problems is that I think I can put off until tomorrow the choices I should make today. Perhaps, but perhaps not. As I grow more desperate, I see that others have given up completely and that I could easily do the same if I don't seize my opportunity now.

> Give me, Lord, the desperation I need to use
> every opportunity to recover from my
> unhealthy behaviors.

REFLECT | *No more treaties with the enemy.*

Day 39 God Is Trustworthy

READ | Deuteronomy 7:9
*Know therefore that the L*ORD *your God is God; he is the faithful God, keeping his covenant of love to a thousand generations of those who love him and keep his commands.*

Part of the reason I trust my strange ways of eating is that I don't trust anything or anyone else. I might have been significantly disappointed by family members; I might have leaned too hard on friends; I might have expected the world to grant me favors. I might have prayed and asked God to deliver me, and it seemed that even God disappointed me.

Now I'm learning that God is trustworthy: "He is the faithful God." No, he doesn't deliver me from my obsession with food or provide a magical wand to make it all go away. But when I lay my needs before him, he doesn't let me down. When I follow his path, he clears the way before me.

God, help me know you as the faithful and
trustworthy being you are, even when I don't
understand what's going on.

REFLECT | *To trust God is to come to know him and feel loved by him.*

Day 40 The Unhurried Recovery

READ | Deuteronomy 7:22
*The L*ORD *your God will drive out those nations before you, little by little. You will not be allowed to eliminate them all at once, or the wild animals will multiply around you.*

I have often wished that God would instantly, miraculously transform me into an angelic person with stable emotions, tamed inner drives, and perfect behavior. Then I would have no struggles with eating.

But just as God moved the Israelites slowly into their promised land, God moves me slowly through the growing process.

My setbacks and struggles are not lost moments. As long as I'm making progress, I'm claiming new territory. Little by little, I can express my emotions in more appropriate ways.

This slow, steady progress keeps the "wild animals" away. I don't transfer my obsessiveness to compulsive spending, sexual fantasies, or workaholic highs to manage the pain. I give it all up.

Thank you, God, for the small amount of progress
each day even when I can't see it.

REFLECT | *God sets the pace of my journey.*

Day 41 Using All the Tools

READ | Deuteronomy 8:1

Be careful to follow every command I am giving you today, so that you may live and increase and may enter and possess the land that the LORD promised.

Because I still have to eat to live, it's easy to pretend I'm not angry so I don't have to write about it in my journal or talk to a friend about it or pray about it. But I watch my food portions get a little too big or too small.

The journey of surrendering an eating problem is a lot like the Israelites' quest to possess the promised land. They had to be freed from the Egyptians, they had to cross the Red Sea, and they had to wander. I have Red Seas to cross and wanderings to endure. I can't neglect any of the footwork.

I want to fully possess the promised land, so I'm going to follow every command every day and use every tool. The tools that make me squirm are usually the ones I need the most. When I use all of them, the journey to wholeness is rich with blessing.

> Thank you, God, for the tools that help me
> "possess the land"! Help me not to neglect
> any of them.

REFLECT | *The tools I fear using are the ones I need to use.*

Day 42 Feeding on the Truth

)READ | Deuteronomy 8:3

He humbled you, causing you to hunger and then feeding you with manna . . . to teach you that man does not live on bread alone but on every word that comes from the mouth of the LORD.

My quest for wholeness sometimes causes me to hunger physically for food and emotionally for control. When these hungers flare up, I can choose not to feed on food or the excessive denial of it, but on manna, the spiritual principles of God:

- God loves me;
- God sees my value when others around me do not;

■ God is working in me to bring out positive qualities and capabilities in me I never thought were possible.

In spite of my disappointments, my frustrations, and my anger, I accept the truth of these principles. Slowly they become part of me through prayer, journaling, meditation, and service.

Teach me, God, to depend on you instead of food.

REFLECT | *Seeking God fills my inner and outer hunger.*

Day 43 The Plentiful Land of Wholeness

READ | Deuteronomy 8:7, 9
For the LORD your God is bringing you into a good land . . . a land where bread will not be scarce and you will lack nothing.

It is tempting to view eating sensibly as a dry land of nothingness because I can't overindulge or plot ways to become thin. But it is not a barren land, but rather an exciting, prosperous one.

As I adjust to a normal level of hunger, I discover that I lack nothing. So much fills my life because I am facing my defects of character. Because I'm learning how to handle my jealousy and fear of intimacy, my relationships are improving. Because I'm not so afraid of failure, my daily tasks are becoming interesting puzzles. I'm forgiving others and releasing the problems of my past. I'm making new and better goals because I see my value and believe in myself. I feel inner fulfillment because I am confident that God loves me no matter how much I weigh.

Help me to trust that wholeness
in body, soul, and spirit
is a better place in life.

REFLECT | *Life can be filled with all the good things I missed
when I was obsessed with food and thinness.*

Day 44 Opening My Hand to Others

READ | Deuteronomy 15:7–8
*If there is a poor man among your brothers . . . be openhanded and
freely lend him whatever he needs.*

There is a panicky tightfistedness about an eating
problem. I can't let go of my food or the money I need
to buy the food. Because I've become so preoccupied with
myself, I feel insecure and squelch any generous feelings I
may have.

As I surrender this whole area of my life I feel so
grateful to God and to others who understand that I am
loosening my grip a little on life. I find I'm a little more
openhanded. I handle money better. I'm more touched by
the needs of others, and I want to share my resources more
with the needy. I become as excited about giving as I am
about receiving.

God, please use me as an instrument of your
openhandedness.

REFLECT | *Generosity grows out of gratefulness.*

Day 45 Changing from Within

R E A D | Joshua 1:8

Do not let this Book of the Law depart from your mouth; meditate on it day and night, so that you may be careful to do everything written in it.

My old fears and negative attitudes linger. Could I have them surgically removed, or would I change if I ripped out Bible pages and ate them in a sandwich?

No, but I can meditate. I can read a verse or two of Scripture, close my eyes, and ask myself a few questions:

What difference does this verse make to me?

What would I do if I were to put this into action?

What is God trying to get through to me?

As I absorb the verses and wait, sometimes I sense a rush of feeling—a release of anger or frustration. At other times I get an idea about something I should do. Still other times nothing happens. But always I thank God for his abiding presence, and that is enough.

As I meditate on your words, God,
help me to be renewed.

R E F L E C T | *Meditation penetrates beyond the mind into the will and the heart.*

Day 46 Celebrating My Progress!

R E A D | Joshua 4:21–22

[Joshua] said to the Israelites, "In the future when your descendants ask their fathers, 'What do these stones mean?' tell them, 'Israel crossed the Jordan on dry ground.'"

The Israelites built memorials to recall their victories and defeats. I have some memorials, too. Here are some of them:

- a bent and yellowed recipe card for chocolate cheesecake that I used to make often and well;
- a half shelf of diet books that now read like a foreign language to me;
- a stained, baggy sweatshirt I used to cover up overweight and underweight;
- journals full of true confessions.

These mementos remind me of how far I've progressed and the bondage from which I've escaped.

Help me, God, not to forget how far I've come, no matter how far that is or isn't.

R E F L E C T | *I am becoming a different person.*

Day 47 Procrastinating

R E A D | Joshua 18:3

So Joshua said to the Israelites: "How long will you wait before you begin to take possession of the land that the LORD, the God your fathers, has given you?"

"I have to wait until I'm in a better place in life. . . ."

When I say these words, am I waiting for a better life or a fantastic life? It is not going to come.

If I regret anything about changing my direction and going toward eating sensibly and living well it's that I waited so long to begin it, that I stalled so long on plateaus, that I haven't used the tools more often. While I stood in the waiting rooms (and perhaps some of that waiting was necessary), I hurt myself and many other people. I cannot take that back, but I can remain serious about my progress today.

> Thank you, God, for my progress,
> and nudge me out of my waiting rooms.

REFLECT | *To put off growth is to put off having a better life.*

Day 48 Doubts and Questions

READ | Judges 6:13

"But sir," said Gideon, "if the LORD is with us, why has all this happened to us? Where are all his wonders that our fathers told us about . . ."

Can you imagine asking an angel of the Lord the questions Gideon asked? Most people think it's wrong to question God as Gideon did, but God (through the angel) told Gideon, "Go in the strength you have. . . ." (v. 14). Then God commissioned Gideon to save Israel. Apparently, God didn't think Gideon was wrong to ask questions.

As eating in a less erratic way causes my buried feelings to surface, I need to get all my cards of confusion, doubt, and bitterness on the table and examine them. Am I mad at

God? Do I doubt his love for me? Where was he during my childhood trauma?

I may not get answers I fully understand by 5:00 PM. the same day, and I don't have to. But I do need to present them to him. Then he can answer them in his timing, and I know I'm accepted by the one I desperately need.

> Lord, I love you, but I get frustrated
> with the way things happen. Show me how
> to resolve that.

REFLECT | *I can feel safe enough with God to question him.*

Day 49 How Spiritual Friends Help

READ | Ruth 1:16

But Ruth replied, "Don't urge me to leave you or to turn back from you. Where you go I will go, and where you stay I will stay. Your people will be my people and your God my God."

As a young widow, Ruth no doubt felt broken and aimless. She followed the comings and goings of her mother-in-law, in spite of their religious and cultural gaps. She even adopted Naomi's faith.

This is similar to what happens between friends and members of my support group. By asking a friend to help me, I am saying:

- Show me how to start over.
- Show me how to mend my brokenness.
- Help me break out of my isolation.
- Show me that you accept me.
- Show me how your faith works.
- Warn me if I get off track.

As I help others, I have the honor of doing these things.

Help me choose a friend who will be open and honest with me, someone I can learn from. Help me not to lean on superficial relationships.

REFLECT | *A friend shows me what I need to do to progress and what I am not doing to progress.*

Day 50   Rooting Out the Pain

READ | 1 Samuel 1:15
Hannah replied, "I am a woman who is deeply troubled. I have not been drinking wine or beer; I was pouring out my soul to the LORD.*"*

Hannah responded to the pain of childlessness by pouring out her soul to the Lord. She prayed with such feeling that the priest thought she was drunk. What a healthy release for grief and frustration.

The same frustrations that drive me to overeat and undereat drive me to pour out my soul to the Lord. As I pray this way, I release, instead of hoarding; I feel, instead of numbing out; I touch someone, instead of withdrawing; I know his presence, instead of remaining in my own loneliness.

God, I want to be willing to show my true self to you without shame or embarrassment.

REFLECT | *I can trust God enough to pour out my soul to him.*

Day 51 Brokenness Gives Life

READ | 1 Samuel 2:6
The LORD brings death and makes alive; he brings down to the grave and raises up.

I welcome my pain and desperation because they force me to examine myself and come clean. They bring forth life.

I feel so miserable that I gather up my courage, set aside my pride, and admit to someone else that I have been dishonest and conceited. Then this person thanks me, saying, "You have named my problem for me. I see it all now and I want to change, just like you said." This person's brokenness speaks to mine and we are a team. We form a strong friendship and continue to share our stories.

I'm glad I've surrendered to this death of myself. Without it, I would not have found life.

Help me, God, to accept your way of bringing me new life from my brokenness.

REFLECT | *I can admit my brokenness in many ways without shame.*

Day 52 Principles Before Personalities

READ | 1 Samuel 8:6
But when they said, "Give us a king to lead us," this displeased Samuel; so he prayed to the LORD.

When I let my behavior hinge on one person ("a king to lead us"), I place personalities before principles. This happens when I lean on others to make me feel OK.

Changing my behavior regarding food is based on the principles of God and on God himself. I surrender to God, not to someone else. I get through tough times because God provides me with help through others and through tools I use by myself such as prayer, meditation, Scripture reading, and journaling. I establish and strengthen my relationship with God. It is God who sustains me and can never fail me.

> Help me, God, not to lean too heavily on
> others or to allow their mistakes to create
> problems for me.

REFLECT | *My choice to abstain does not depend on the successes and failures of others.*

Day 53 No Longer Hiding

READ | 1 Samuel 12:20
You have done all this evil; yet do not turn away from the LORD, *but serve the* LORD *with all your heart.*

It's tough to go back to a support group after I've failed again. It's tough to admit to anyone that I've exaggerated; it's tough to pray after I've blown up at my kids. I think God (and probably everyone else) is disgusted with me because I goofed.

When I want to run and hide, I need to come out and show my face. God may or may not be disgusted with me, but he still loves me and wants me to turn to him. The others will handle it the best they can.

I'm learning to stand up instead of hide and to get those unbearable moments over with when I'd like to put them off indefinitely. The results are usually not as bad as I imagine them to be, and I find a sense of healing from owning up to my faults and starting over.

Help me, God, to learn to come to you when I goof.

REFLECT | *When I want to hide from God, I need him the most.*

Day 54 Achieving Importance

READ | 1 Samuel 13:14

. . . the LORD has sought out a man after his own heart and appointed him leader of his people, because you have not kept the LORD's command.

My culture convinces me that I cannot be outstanding or influential unless I am good-looking, well-educated, or highly skilled. King Saul was at least two of these. He was physically appealing (a head taller than others) and a brave, successful warrior. Why would God replace this statuesque man with David, an unknown keeper of smelly sheep? Saul lacked something important that David the shepherd had: David was a man after God's own heart.

In the past, I felt ineffective no matter how hard I tried or how good I looked. I was never good enough. Now I no longer care about being outstanding or influential; I want to seek after God, and I trust that he gives me whatever significance and influence he wants me to have.

I seek after you, God. I no longer concern
myself with being outstanding and influential.

REFLECT | *It's what I seek in life, not how I look, that gives me significance.*

Day 55 Surviving Rejection

READ | 1 Samuel 15:10

Then the word of the LORD came to Samuel: "I am grieved that I have made Saul king, because he has turned away from me and has not carried out my instructions."

Even God gets rejected. When Saul passed over God, God grieved, but he also moved on, asking Samuel to appoint another king.

I'm learning that I can choose how I wish to respond to being dismissed. I don't have to assume that others think I'm a worthless person. I don't have to jump on my high horse and scorn the other person forever.

Like God, I can grieve and go on. I may understand the rejection better as time passes. I may see how I unintentionally hurt that person, or I may learn that their objections had little to do with me and everything to do with things they were going through. And when I am at fault, I can choose to learn from my mistakes.

God, help me get through rejection and go on.
Help me not take it personally.

REFLECT | *Rejection doesn't have to cripple me.*

Day 56 Mood-Swing Mania

READ | 1 Samuel 15:22

To obey is better than sacrifice.

"Let me make it up to you!" I used to say. As long as I was following the dictates of my demands and cravings and living in my feelings, I found it impossible to be kind to people on a regular basis. It was much easier to withdraw or to be harsh or hypersensitive. I said a lot of things I didn't mean. Then when my negative mood was over, I was ready to make it up to whomever I'd harmed.

Nothing replaces simply being kind in the first place. No one enjoyed my emotional roller coasters. Now I find that I don't enjoy them either.

I'd much rather *obey* by straightening out my attitude now, so I don't have to *sacrifice* by worrying about how I'll make it up to someone for being so unkind, grouchy, or lazy.

God, live in me and through me so I can learn
to be kind on a regular basis.

REFLECT | *Preventing a bad mood works better than making up for one.*

Day 57 Looks Can Be Defeating

READ | 1 Samuel 16:7
Man looks at the outward appearance, but the LORD looks at the heart.

My outward appearance has been the downer in my life for a long time. I was never thin enough; when I weighed the right amount, I was never proportioned correctly; even when I thought I looked good, my face was such an odd shape!

As I move through life, my belief that God loves me grows; this helps me accept my body, my face, and my normal shape (even though some would say the last item

44

resembles a pear). There are still days when no matter how skillfully I apply makeup and how deftly I work with my hair, I don't look good enough to suit myself. So I remind myself that I'm OK. I lean forward and whisper to the face in the mirror, "Hello, world. This is me. This face is as good as it's going to get, and that's OK! OK?"

> Steep me in your love and all the nurturing
> that it brings, and let it soak through to my
> flagging self-esteem.

REFLECT | *Because God looks on my heart with mercy, I can learn to look at my outward appearance with mercy.*

Day 58 Living in the Extremes

READ | 1 Samuel 22:8
Is that why you have all conspired against me? No one tells me. . . . None of you. . . .

These extreme words—all, no one, none—were the words of a near madman, King Saul, who slaughtered the people to whom he spoke these words. The excessive tendency is toward all or nothing, black or white.

I am learning to think and do things in moderation, and that feels uncomfortable at first. . . . No matter how much I adore people, they are not one hundred percent wonderful. Some people insist that carbohydrates are bad, but they're part of a balanced diet.

Moderation is full of paradoxes! There is some good in the worst of us and some bad in the best of us. I don't have to rage; I can be moderately angry and cope with it. I don't have to panic or withdraw; I can stay with my uneasiness and let it pass.

Thank you, Lord, for leading me away from the
extreme paths in life.

REFLECT | *I don't have to live out on the edge anymore; I can enjoy balance and moderation in life.*

Day 59 Stormy Relationships

READ | 1 Samuel 24:10
Some urged me to kill you, but I spared you; I said, "I will not lift my hand against my master, because he is the Lord's anointed."

David had several reasons to kill Saul. First, Saul had tried to kill him a few times. Second, David had been anointed as king to replace Saul because Saul had rejected God. Yet David did not take revenge or even come close to it.

Revenge is God's instrument, but I justify my vengeful attempts because I use benign weapons such as gossip and exaggeration. If I get serious about revenge, I may even use sarcastic jibes, or I may withdraw from the relationship.

I'm learning to lay down my weapons and try to reconcile troublesome relationships. When that doesn't work, all I can do is lay the relationship before God and say, "I have done what I can do. I surrender it to you. Fix it when the time is right."

God, help me reconcile with others
instead of taking revenge.

REFLECT | *I can let God tend to God's business.*

Day 60 Choosing Camaraderie

READ | 1 Samuel 31:4

Saul said to his armor-bearer, "Draw your sword and run me through, or these uncircumcised fellows will come and run me through and abuse me." But his armor-bearer was terrified and would not do it; so Saul took his own sword and fell on it.

Suicide seems like an escape, but it is the ultimate unhealthy isolation. Isolation didn't help me with my eating problem. Occasionally I find myself toying with unhealthy thoughts, but I choose now to talk to someone instead. I choose camaraderie over isolation.

Camaraderie helps me because it gives me the perspective I need. In my isolation, I become like Saul, projecting the worst possible result in every situation. The more I think about it, the more hopeless I feel. The camaraderie of a telephone call, or a support-group meeting, or pouring out my soul to God awakens me out of my isolated stupor and shakes me into remembering that with God there is always hope.

Please rescue me, God, when I lose sight
of the miraculous hope available in you.

REFLECT | *I can choose fellowship with those who understand me, over self-destructive thoughts.*

Day 61 Confrontation Palpitations

READ | 2 Samuel 12:7

Then Nathan said to David, "You are the man!"

Not every accusation that's been made about me was true, but some have been true. When I'm confronted, I usually tell the person that I will consider their words and get back to them. If I try to respond immediately, I either defend myself or I take all the blame. I have no objectivity until the rush of embarrassment dies down. Then I can see if it's true, and if it is, I can admit that to myself, to God, and to my friend.

Not everyone confronts me as directly as Nathan confronted David. One friend may tell another how disgusting it is that I scarf down my food. I may be embarrassed for days because I know it's true. By the time I share it with a support group, I say, "This friend was right. I do scarf down my food. "

God, please help me listen to those who confront me, even if it's unpleasant.

REFLECT | *I may learn more from friends' harsh, confrontive words than from their kind ones.*

Day 62 Wrong? Not Me!

READ | 2 Samuel 12:13
Then David said to Nathan, "I have sinned against the LORD. "

For years I couldn't admit I was wrong, and I hid my faults, just as David hid his affair with Bathsheba. Their deception cost Bathsheba's husband his life, just as my unacknowledged faults caused my friends and family to suffer.

It may be difficult to admit I'm wrong, but it's even more difficult to keep up the facade of being right because I have to keep rationalizing my behavior and reviewing my defense. I miss out on a lot of warmth and fun because I have to keep a distance that reminds everyone that I was right. That can be exhausting.

When I admit I'm wrong as David did, I feel relieved. There is no shame in being human and making mistakes. There may be consequences, but God is gracious; I can always start over.

Give me the courage and sense of security in your love to admit my faults.

REFLECT | *It is a sign of strength to admit I am wrong.*

Day 63 Go Where the Love Is

READ | 2 Samuel 19:6
You love those who hate you and hate those who love you.

To prove myself I have tried to win over those who do not like me. Proving myself is important only when I think poorly of myself. I spent a lot of time trying to impress them and feeling bad because they prefer others over me. The craziness of my compulsive nature means that I also treat those I love poorly because I take them for granted. They don't benefit from my best behavior, but they suffer with my worst.

The saying "Go where the love is" means that I should enjoy people who like me and not worry about everyone else. I'm learning to accept that the relationships I have are enough; actually, they're plenty! If I am going to be friends with someone who currently doesn't like me, it will happen. I don't have to chase it.

Thank you for those who like me, God.
Open my eyes to their needs and delights.

R E F L E C T | *God provides the relationships I need. My job is to give to those relationships.*

Day 64   Just One Hero

R E A D | 2 Samuel 22:17
He reached down from on high and took hold of me; he drew me out of deep waters.

Ultimately, every person on this earth will fail or disappoint me because they're only human. I've had such fears of abandonment that I've expected my parents, my sibling, my friends, and my spouse to be everything I need. When any of them disappointed me, I looked for comfort (or was it revenge?) in my overeating.

No one can truly rescue me but God. Bible passages such as today's portray God as some kind of hero out of the old West or from an exotic space adventure who draws me out of deep trouble just in the nick of time. God is the one who comes for me and helps me. He's the only one who can legitimately take that responsibility, because only he is divinely equipped to do so.

God, I look to you to be God to me.

R E F L E C T | *I can let friends be friends and God be the one who rescues me.*

Day 65 More Open Spaces

R E A D | 2 Samuel 22:20a

He brought me out into a spacious place.

Wholeness feels like a spacious place because I can breathe deeply and relax so easily. I don't feel so tense because I'm no longer conniving or obsessing about food. I'm not so needy, and I don't have to prove anything to anyone.

My choices are no longer limited. I can pick up and go somewhere at the last minute without wondering what I'll eat, if I'll like it enough, and when I'll exercise. I'm free to gratefully eat whatever meal is put in front of me.

My heart and mind are more spacious, too. Listening to others share their struggles opens me to people I would have otherwise rejected. I see how wrong I've been about people and how much I have to learn.

Help me to relax in this spacious place, God.

R E F L E C T | *I have many choices and I can enjoy them.*

Day 66 Worth Rescuing

R E A D | 2 Samuel 22:20b

He rescued me because he delighted in me.

Many people put up with me; some enjoy me; others even admire me. But God is the one who delights in me.

Yes, I make mistakes, but God delights in me.

Yes, I'm a compulsive eater-spender-volunteer, but God still delights in me.

Yes, I hurt people's feelings, but God keeps delighting in me.

Yes, I fall short of my potential at times, but God continues to delight in me.

Yes, I forget to delight in his presence, but God doesn't stop delighting in me.

I'm not a second-best kid with God, no matter what I've done or what's happened to me. I'm always first rate.

Thank you, God, that you delight in someone as flawed and broken as me.

R E F L E C T | *God not only loves me, God likes me.*

ꟼDay 67 Doing My Part

R E A D | 2 Samuel 24:24
I insist on paying you for it. I will not sacrifice to the Lord my God burnt offerings that cost me nothing.

I'm asking myself less frequently, "How little can I get by with?" The integrity and rigorous honesty required on this journey stirs in me the desire to do my part. Friends talk about how they refuse to do shoddy work and how they no longer feel comfortable stealing time from their employers. They want to honor God by offering him work that costs them effort. Their example shows me that the softer, easier, lazier way of my culture offers only guilt and shame.

As a result, I am no longer interested in how much I can get out of someone or how little I can spend for a quality service. I feel cheapened by uneven relationships in which

I do more taking than giving. I like wanting to do the best I can by others. That feels good.

God, please help me escape the free-lunch mentality.

REFLECT | *I want to offer to God and to others the best I can give.*

Day 68 Making Decisions

READ | 1 Kings 3:9
So give your servant a discerning heart to govern your people and to distinguish between right and wrong.

Should I tell the truth if it hurts someone? If I try to help this person, will it increase their problems? What is a fair consequence for my child's misbehavior?

As my journey continues, I think more clearly. I'm not making decisions based on how I can get my inflated needs met or on what people will think of me if I do certain things.

When faced with a difficult decision or judgment, that inner serenity kicks in, and I brainstorm ideas for handling the situation. As I wait, the answers usually come to me. These decisions used to baffle me, but I sense that my God-given intuition is returning. I'm learning to trust myself again.

God, help me continue to sort out my priorities and motives so I can make wise decisions.

REFLECT | *As I dismantle the old negative tapes in my head, I can get in touch with my healthy decision-making capabilities.*

Day 69 Rest Therapy

READ | 1 Kings 19:4–5
"I have had enough, Lord," [Elijah] said. 'Take my life; I am no better than my ancestors!" Then he lay down under the tree and fell asleep.

Because food made me feel good, I thought I was invincible. If I was sick, I got up, went to work, came home, and did routine chores. The drivenness behind the eating permeated every area of my life. I needed to prove that I was good enough, better and stronger than others.

When Elijah, a prophet of great faith, became discouraged he got away from it all. He poured his heart out to God and he took a nap. A little later, an angel awakened him and fed him, and then he rested again.

It's OK for me to rest or to take a day off when I'm exhausted. Living well has to be part of my daily life as much as eating sensibly.

Help me to take good care of myself.

REFLECT | *God wants me to have proper rest and refreshment.*

Day 70 The Power of Gentleness

READ | 1 Kings 19:12
After the earthquake came a fire, but the Lord was not in the fire. And after the fire came a gentle whisper.

God was not in the wind, earthquake, or fire, but he was in the gentle whisper of all things.

I want to show God's mighty gentleness to myself. I'm not the best-looking person in the world, but I'm still loved. I'm not completing this new task on time, but that's normal with new tasks.

Gentleness is a quality that I have undervalued and underestimated. It has so much power behind it. When I speak gently, my angry child gives up that venom. When I look gently at my friend, she releases the full force of her frustration, cleansing her jagged emotions. When I speak a soft phrase, my spouse sets his self-esteem back on the road to restoration.

God, teach me to handle myself and others with the gentleness you use with me.

R E F L E C T | *A soft smile can often accomplish what a shout cannot.*

Day 71 Releasing the Secrets

R E A D | 2 Kings 17:9
The Israelites secretly did things against the LORD their God that were not right.

Eating by myself outfoxes others. No one knows how much or how little I eat. Eating a sandwich before meeting someone for lunch helped me look controlled as I ordered a small salad or a glass of iced tea. People never knew about the way I pinched food here and there, about my hourly snacks or my sweet-tooth binges. It was my secret life.

"We're as sick as our secrets," goes the saying. Israel never faced her secrets, and within a few years she was scattered and lost in history. I need to share my disgusting eating patterns and the lengths to which I've gone to get junk food. I need to tell how much or how little I've weighed and how I feel about that. In releasing these secrets, I find relief. As my capacity to be rigorously honest grows, so do I.

Help me see that secrecy is what gives my secrets their
power and that when I share them,
they become harmless.

REFLECT | *I can share my secrets and know that I am still loved.*

Day 72 Mixed Truth

READ | 2 Kings 17:33
They worshiped the Lord, but they also served their own gods in accordance with the customs of the nations from which they had been brought.

It's easy to mix the truth with popular ideas of my culture. When we deal with an issue as basic as eating we can fool ourselves in many ways. I need to be vigilant about living in the truth and not giving into fad-dieting. This also includes not allowing my eating problems to take over my life. My attention needs to be on God, not on me.

The road to wholeness is not about conquering, gaining self-control, and becoming sufficient. It's about surrendering myself to God.

The truth works. I won't compromise it.

God, reveal to me my legalistic practices, quick fixes,
and egotistical ideas.

REFLECT | *I can listen to others' ideas and test them against God's basic requirement of me: surrender.*

Day 73 Unmasking God

READ | 1 Chronicles 16:11
Look to the LORD and his strength; seek his face always.

"Seek his face" is such a mystical and religious-sounding phrase. How does someone do this?

Seek? I have let my obsession with food block out God's presence and assistance. I must reacquaint myself with him.

His face? I seek not only God, but his face. I discover who God is behind all those masks I've put on him—policeman, Santa Claus, bellhop. I find that he is the divine parent who cares so much for me that he sacrificed his own child to make things right.

Always? God cannot be absorbed in a year, ten years, or a hundred years. Seeking God is a lifetime task, but an enjoyable one!

God, I want to seek you and quit seeing you with the masks I've placed on you.

REFLECT | *Even after I find God, I go on seeking him.*

Day 74 Discouraging Influences

READ | Ezra 4:4
Then the peoples around them set out to discourage the people of Judah and make them afraid to go on [re]building [the temple].

People have discouraged me in my journey to wholeness. Friends with whom I used to eat compulsively have made fun of my "new thing." People with whom I have been enmeshed have not liked it that I am developing my own identity and do not share every secret with them. Even some of those to whom I've made amends do not talk to me. I'm baffled at times, but I refuse to worry about them.

I pray that these people will accept my new attitudes, but I can't let their lack of acceptance distract me. I can't change others, but I can, with God's help, change myself, and that is what is happening. I have been waiting for this change all my life. I feel free to know and love God, to know and love others.

> God, please tame the tongues of those
> who discourage me.

REFLECT | *I can't change others' opinions of me, but I can refuse to give their opinions power over me.*

↙Day 75 Sharing from the Gut

READ | Ezra 10:1

While Ezra was praying and confessing, weeping and throwing himself down before the house of God, a large crowd . . . gathered around him. They too wept bitterly.

The difference between a humdrum support-group meeting and a boldly empowering one is rigorous honesty. When others confess and humble themselves, I feel safe enough to do the same. The power of others' honesty nearly bounces off me, empowering me to be honest myself. I feel safe in this kind of group, because whatever I say will be accepted.

Gradually I'm learning to share myself even in meetings where people aren't so boldly honest. Even then, I can share my secrets and confess my sick behaviors and defects of character. I do this for myself, but the power will bounce off others as well.

Thank you for support-group meetings, God. Help me share myself as honestly as possible.

REFLECT | *I can use each support-group meeting to advance my journey.*

Day 76 Good Grieving

READ | Nehemiah 1:4
When I heard these things, I sat down and wept. For some days I mourned and fasted and prayed before the God of heaven.

Grieving is good for me. If I had fully faced my grief, I would not have had to use an eating disorder to calm myself. Now I find myself grieving over past hurts I've never faced, over my defects of character, over catastrophic world events, over friends who were abused as children.

If my friend tells me she's moving away, I celebrate with her if she's happy, but I cry in front of her, too. I need to show her how I will miss her presence, and she needs to see how much she means to me.

Grieving isn't weak. Nehemiah, a shrewd politician who worked in the court of the Persian empire, sat in the ruins of his homeland and grieved over its destruction. Then he went on to lead a movement to rebuild it. That is how change begins.

I surrender all my grief to you, Lord, along with my
need to look strong.

REFLECT | *I can grieve when I feel the need to do so.*

Day 77 Gathered, Not Scattered

READ | Nehemiah 1:8–9

*If you are unfaithful, I will scatter you among the nations, but if
you return to me and obey my commands, then . . . I will gather them
from there and bring them to the place I have chosen. . . .*

Scattered thoughts and feelings have preceded my epi-
sodes with obsessing on food. I feel aimless, and I want so
many things that I want nothing. My drivenness has forced
me to choose my most urgent need: to overeat, diet, look
good, or succeed.

Scattering has been a curse on nations throughout
history, and I can see why. I feel miserable when I'm scattered inside. Gathering again healed a nation's curse, and
my recovery allows God to gather me again. Being gathered
helps me focus on specific purposes and push away my
drivenness to overeat or undereat. I experience some of my
most content moments when I gather myself before God. I
center myself on him, and we both know I am headed for
health and wholeness in him.

Gather together the scattered parts of me,
and draw me to yourself, God.

REFLECT | *The feeling of scatteredness can leave me.*

Day 78 Facing Authority Figures

R E A D | Nehemiah 2:2–3

I was very much afraid, but I said to the king, ". . . why should my face not look sad when the city where my fathers are buried lies in ruins?"

Power struggles with authority figures or feelings of having to appease them create inner turmoil that lures me into thoughts of food. When there's a great stone face on a supervisor at work, a committee chairperson, or the manager of a store in which I wish to return an item, I feel there is no way to get through to them. So I react by either coming on too strong or becoming a wimp, then munching out or refusing to eat.

No more. Since I've tried to quit blaming, complaining, and people pleasing, I can now listen to their concerns, state my concerns, and negotiate. Even if nothing works, I have the satisfaction of knowing I'm behaving like a problem solver. I no longer let these situations ruin my life by responding with compulsive behavior.

God, please give me understanding, tact, and creativity
to deal with each authority figure in my life.

R E F L E C T | *I can respond to authority figures without getting upset.*

Day 79 Farewell, Rescuer

READ | Nehemiah 2:12–13
I had not told anyone what my God had put in my heart to do for Jerusalem. . . . By night I went out . . . examining the walls of Jerusalem, which had been broken down. . . .

News flash: I don't have to rescue the world. Now when I think God is putting something in my heart to do, I try to make sure it's from God and not from my egotistical need to rescue. Now I don't rush in so quickly. I wait and pray and try to determine what God wants me to do. Like Nehemiah, who went poking around in the night, I investigate first. I may not even tell anyone what I'm up to. Or I may run the idea past someone who understands the situation better.

The results of this cautious but God-driven approach are astounding. I don't burn out, I give my whole heart to something with no regret, and I don't expect results or gratefulness. That's because I'm doing it for God and not for anyone else. He supplies the energy, results, and solutions.

Please show me the ways you want me to serve you,
God, and how to approach them.

REFLECT | *I can carefully choose the ways I will serve God passionately.*

Day 80 Is There Rubble in My Life?

READ | Nehemiah 4:10
Meanwhile, the people in Judah said, "The strength of the laborers is giving out, and there is so much rubble that we cannot rebuild the wall."

Some seemingly innocent behaviors, which I once thought were allowable for me, were really only rubble. They put me in slippery situations that call for such strength that I lose or barely maintain my balance. Usually I am more deeply attached to these behaviors than I would like to admit. Can I keep potato chips in my house without obsessing on them? Am I drinking too many diet sodas? Am I overexercising? Are my meal portions larger or smaller than they need to be?

These are the tough questions I must ask myself in order to clear away the rubble. Only as I do that can I rebuild my food habits from the inside out.

Help me surrender my rubble behaviors so I can pursue my journey into wholeness.

REFLECT | *I can clear away rubble behaviors, even if that doesn't make sense to others.*

Day 81 Justice in All My Dealings

READ | Nehemiah 5:9, 11
So I continued, "What you are doing is not right. . . . Give back to them immediately their fields, vineyards, olive groves, and houses."

In the past I was honest—when a sales clerk gave me incorrect extra change, I gave it back. But I was dishonest in other ways. I blamed others for my problems and made excuses for my weight difficulties.

Because I wasn't rigorously honest, I didn't insist that others deal with me in just ways. I knew I wasn't playing it exactly straight, so why should they have to?

Now that I'm working on becoming rigorously honest, I'm less afraid to ask people who intimidate me or people I love if things are fair. I'm not policing others' morals, but I'm also not afraid to stand up for myself in a candid, polite way. Honesty is no longer such a scary thing to me.

God, help me deal truthfully with others and ask them to do the same with me.

REFLECT | *Being honest about myself makes me less afraid to ask others to be honest.*

Day 82 Apologies Don't Go On Forever

READ | Nehemiah 8:9–10
All the people had been weeping as they listened to the words of the Law. Nehemiah said, . . . "Do not grieve, for the joy of the LORD is your strength."

I have cried over the way I've dealt with myself, my friends, and my family in the past. In my drivenness, I have ignored them and judged them without mercy. Once I've surrendered and made amends, it's time to surrender my guilt, too. Apologizing over and over doesn't help; it makes everyone feel worse.

It's time for restoration. I can celebrate and be happy. God is showing me my defects of character, and he will change me if I keep surrendering them to him. It's time to be grateful for what God is doing in my life. This leads me to surrender more of myself to God.

You are my strength,
and I am glad that I have surrendered to you.

REFLECT | *Restoration is better than regret.*

Day 83 Fear of Success?

READ | Esther 2:7, 17

Esther . . . was lovely in form and features. Now the king was attracted to Esther more than to any of the other women. . . . So he set a royal crown on her head and made her queen. . . .

What terrible things will happen to me if I look attractive? Will I be swept away by a tyrant who drinks too much? That's what happened to the young Jewish girl, Esther. With God's strength, she confronted this tyrant-king when doing so meant saving her people, even though she feared for her life.

I won't face a tyrant-king, but I have challenges of my own: Can I be comfortable with myself at a normal weight? Can I handle situations I haven't had to face before?

I can do these things if I surrender each scary feeling and situation to God. I can do them if I continue to rely on the strength of others like me. I can do them if I get excited about God's purposes for me instead of being obsessed with my fears.

I surrender my fears to you,
and I ask you to use me
in dynamic ways for your causes.

REFLECT | *I don't have to be afraid to face my fears when I step onto the scale!*

Day 84 Feel Pretty? Pretty Awful!

R E A D | Esther 2:12

. . . she had to complete twelve months of beauty treatments pre-scribed for the women, six months with oil of myrrh and six with perfumes and cosmetics.

Is it OK for me to try to look attractive? Is it a worthwhile effort to do what I can with what I have?

Some of Esther's girlfriends must have clucked their tongues about the excessiveness of twelve months of beauty treatments. But Esther followed this beauty pageant regimen because her mentor-cousin advised her to do so. It turned out to be God's will, and Esther saved her people.

What is God's will for my appearance? It isn't overatten-tion to it as it was for Esther, but it doesn't mean neglecting myself or looking dowdy, either. I am growing more com-fortable with the appearance that God gave me, and I pay attention to it without overdoing it. I enjoy making myself as easy on the other person's eyes as possible.

I surrender my appearance to you, God, and I ask you
to help me cultivate a healthy attitude about it.

R E F L E C T | *God will not abandon me because of my weight, and I can have fun trying to look attractive.*

Day 85 Expectations of God

R E A D | Job 1:20–22

*At this, Job got up and tore his robe . . . and said: ". . . the L*ORD* gave and the L*ORD* has taken away; may the name of the L*ORD* be praised."
In all this, Job did not sin by charging God with wrongdoing.*

When crises occur in my life, I realize that I expected certain things of God, such as decent food, clothing, and shelter; a family that loves me and doesn't get into trouble; a job I like; neighbors that don't play loud music all night; minor sicknesses only; eighty years of life. When these expectations are not fulfilled, I become bitter.

As I hear the stories of others with eating problems and as I attempt to eat sensibly, I become more grateful and humble. This affects my relationship with God so that I'm less likely to make demands on him and charge him with wrongdoing. I'm more likely to surrender my expectations of God to God and accept and endure problems.

> I come to you, God,
> with gratefulness for what you have
> given me in this life.

REFLECT | *I can stop expecting things from God and become grateful for what I have.*

Day 86 Wordless Comfort

READ | Job 2:13
Then they sat down on the ground with him for seven days and seven nights. No one said a word to him, because they saw how great his suffering was.

When Job lost his children and livestock and was afflicted with disease, his friends came to him and sat in silence with him for the first seven days.

In the past, I frequently offered what I thought were eloquent words of comfort. But in support groups I watch what happens without my eloquent answers ever being vocalized. People find comfort by talking through problems without interruption, by crying without interruption, and by hearing God's promptings themselves.

Perhaps this is what is meant by the term *ministry of presence.* The best comfort I can offer is being with others in their hurt. I can simply say to a grieving person, "Can I sit beside you for a while?" or "Do you want to talk?"

Thank you, God, for your empowering
presence in my life. Help me communicate
that presence to others in grief.

REFLECT | *I can surrender my need to appear eloquent.*

Day 87 Powerlessness Empowers

READ | Job 6:13
Do I have any power to help myself, now that success has been driven from me?

Power is supposedly linked with success, and powerlessness is linked with failure. Powerless people have little to say in politics, economics, or even relationships.

By surrendering my strange ways of eating, I'm agreeing to do an unbelievable thing: to give up power. I admit that I am powerless over my eating problems.

This works because it melts my drivenness to overpower my problems. This drivenness backfired on me and sabotaged success instead of creating it. As I give up my attempts to be powerful, I am free to invite the greatest power of all to take over and to do for me what I cannot do for myself. This is real power.

I surrender to your great power, God, and I give up my
driven attempts to control my life.

REFLECT | *I admit that I am powerless over my eating*
behaviors.

Day 88 To Feel Sad Is to Be Human

READ | Job 7:11
I will speak out in the anguish of my spirit, I will complain in the
bitterness of my soul.

I desperately wanted to stop feeling bad, sad, and mad.
I've overeaten and starved to get rid of those feelings,
but this only buried them. My feelings became bitter in
the depths of my soul, and they ended up paralyzing me
emotionally.

I'm learning that feeling sad is part of being human.
As long I live on earth, it's going to be this way, and there
is no easy escape from sad feelings. I make decisions about
how I will live this prone-to-trouble existence.

I have decided to go through these sad feelings. This
means I will experience them in their full severity, and
I can use tools to process them: journaling, praying, and
calling friends.

God, give me the strength to survive my intense feelings
and remain strong.

REFLECT | *I can now work through sad feelings because I*
have the courage and the tools, and a repaired relationship with
God.

Day 89 When I Least Expect It

READ | Job 9:10

[God] performs wonders that cannot be fathomed, miracles that cannot be counted.

I am learning that I don't have life figured out. When I am sure someone is headed for trouble, they turn around. Just when I've projected that the road ahead will be rough, it isn't. God keeps intervening when I least expect him to do so.

I don't predict the future anymore. God has a thousand unknowns I don't know about. What I think is the worst possible situation may turn out to be the best thing that has happened to me. I'm less sure of myself, but more sure of God. I'm less sure of exactly how I'll cope, but more sure that I eventually will.

God, help me enjoy the ways you work unexpectedly.

REFLECT | *The door is always open for God to do the unexpected.*

Day 90 Put On a Happy Face?

READ | Job 9:27

If I say, "I will forget my complaint, I will change my expression, and smile," I still dread all my sufferings. . . .

People often ask me how I could have been so miserable but seemed so happy. That's easy. I faked it. I denied that my inner pain existed, except when relationships forced me to face it.

I was good at looking good, looking happy, and looking fine. Like Job, I could forget my complaint and smile but still dread my inner suffering. My strange ways of eating facilitated this pseudo-happiness because it numbed my pain.

Now I tell people how I'm really feeling: I'm OK, I'm stressed, I'm "hangin' in there." I feel free to be liked or disliked for who I am, not who I pretend to be. It's important to admit that I don't feel wonderful all the time, so I don't encourage others to put on a false happy face, either.

God, help me become a genuine, authentic person.

REFLECT | *I give up the dishonest image of being perpetually fine.*

Day 91 Lifting up My Head

READ | Job 11:15
Then you will lift up your face without shame; you will stand firm and without fear.

The shame of the way I overate made me silent about my true self. I felt a desperation so quiet that I seemed to do less than exist. I was less than nothing. I hung my head and looked away when people, especially healthy people, looked at me.

By surrendering to God, I'm allowing him to lift the shame from me. As I reach out toward him, I find that I'm standing, even standing firm. I'm not afraid, but I'm confident.

All this happens because I accept that God values me no matter what I do or have done. He loves me beyond anything I can imagine.

Help me understand, God, that you have rescued me
from shame's power.

REFLECT | *As I admit my powerlessness and surrender to God, I am freed of shame.*

Day 92 How Much Advice Is Enough?

READ | Job 12:13

To God belong wisdom and power; counsel and understanding are his.

Contemporary culture turns people into advice junkies. While I should seek the counsel of advisers (Prov. 15:22), I can also overdo it. It is as if I pull up to a filling station and say, "I'll take three how-tos and two formulas."

Counsel is helpful, but at times I lean too heavily on others and I don't seek God's counsel. With all this chitchat, it is easy to talk about problems but do little about them.

For now I can play catch-up with the advice I've been given. I can bring it before God and let him help me figure out how to follow it.

God, help me consider other's advice but to do what I
think you are leading me to do.

REFLECT | *It is my responsibility to weigh advice and follow through as I see fit.*

Day 93 Hitting Bottom

READ | Job 13:15
Though he slay me, yet will I hope in him.

In times of crisis, I have toyed with the thought of giving up on God and forgetting that I ever believed in him. Yet when I'm at my worst, I need God the most.

When I turn to God in crises, I change. I'm more pliable. So if he speaks to me about my compulsive behavior or defects of character, I'm more likely to surrender them because I have nothing to lose.

There is never a good time or place to give up on God. Even in good times, I realize that he is really all I have, and actually, all I need to survive.

God, help me see that I never have to give up on you.

REFLECT | *No matter how cornered I feel, God can sustain me.*

Day 94 Opinions, Anyone?

READ | Job 15:3
Would [a wise man] argue with useless words, with speeches that have no value?

Winning and being right used to mean everything to me. For days afterward, I would dwell on what I should have said to win an argument. What was at stake all those times? Usually, my flagging self-esteem.

My opinions have become less important because I don't have to prove myself anymore. I'm filling that inner vacuum with the assurance that God loves me, with the camaraderie of other stragglers like me, and with the relief that I'm not a terrible person after all.

I may still hold controversial opinions, but I don't have to bless others with them whenever they ask. And when I do give opinions, I can abandon my attorney-like attitudes and leave my hearers free to think whatever they like.

God, I let go of my neediness to be heard. Help me
present my opinions in a congenial way.

REFLECT | *I don't have to take my opinions so seriously.*

Day 95 Mad at God?

READ | Job 15:12–13
Why has your heart carried you away, and why do your eyes flash,
so that you vent your rage against God . . . ?

I, too, have raged against God. I've screamed and yelled. Or, I've vented my anger in more subtle ways by griping about the church or muttering flip, cynical one-liners to God. Or I've raged against him while mistreating my body with food.

I'm learning to ventilate these angry feelings to God in a different way. I write it out in journals, talk it out in support groups, and pray it out (sometimes rather loudly) in private places. Then, after I ventilate, I express my hope and faith that he will do something to rescue me from my anger. I'm beginning to trust that he loves me even when I'm angry, so I tell him that I trust him with as much faith as I can muster.

God, I want to trust you with every
detail of my life, even when I'm angry
about those details!

REFLECT | *I can talk things out with God and reconcile*
with him.

✓Day 96 Enjoying God

READ | Job 22:26
Surely then you will find delight in the Almighty and will lift up
your face to God.

The idea of finding delight in God sounds a little odd.
I've loved God as a child loves a parent, but I can actually
enjoy him, too.

Because I no longer judge myself so harshly, I don't
assume that he's judging me harshly, too. I experience his
grace and mercy from others who have loved me in spite of
the sickest of my behaviors. I see that God loves me in the
same way, and I feel accepted by him.

I'm learning that God is surprising and interesting. I
see all the unexpected, meaningful things that happen to
me as gifts from him. So I thank him for all the attention
he pays to me.

God, I like the idea of enjoying being with you. Help
me to explore that.

REFLECT | *It is possible to enjoy God's presence.*

Day 97 Wisdom Instead of Excess

READ | Job 28:12

But where can wisdom be found? Where does understanding dwell?

I have given up on my old sources of wisdom such as diet cookbooks, dieting books, and exercise manuals. This wisdom did not solve my problems. Neither did the wisdom of friends who told me how pretty I was no matter how much I weighed.

These sources of wisdom may work for others, but they don't work for me. I am driven. Repairs aren't enough.

Even after I declare that I've completely overhauled my attitude, that old mindset calls out in the form of new dieting fads, liquid diets, and exercise gadgets. Once again, I can choose not to make these things a part of my daily life. Wholeness and wellness are dependent on my surrendering my drives to God daily and banding with others like myself. This works, and this I will do.

God, help me to recognize when I'm leaning on my old sources of wisdom, and help me turn to you.

REFLECT | *My old dieting wisdom doesn't work. I surrender it.*

Day 98 Learn by Doing

READ | Job 28:28

. . . to shun evil is understanding.

It is a normal feeling to want to understand things so I ask, how can I lose weight if I'm not following a strict diet?

Why is an eating problem a spiritual issue? (Because it defines who I am, which is a spiritual issue.) Still, these answers may not make sense to me.

Thankfully, I can quit analyzing and just focus on wholeness. As I progress, I make mistakes and discover things for myself. I may hear an insight I've heard many times, but it finally makes sense to me. As I do the footwork, I understand more.

Wholeness can be understood only by doing—shunning my unhealthy ways and seeking God. These things cannot be understood unless I put them into practice.

God, help me shun my former practices so I may understand life better.

REFLECT | *Wholeness is a learn-as-you-grow activity.*

Day 99 A Symbol of Hope

READ | Job 29:24
When I smiled at them, they scarcely believed it; the light of my face was precious to them.

As my eating problems became worse, hope drained out of my life until I forgot what hope felt like. I wanted hope, but it was so intangible, so elusive, so feeling-oriented. I had trouble being hopeful.

The smile of friends has become a symbol of hope. I see a rush of joy on their faces as they see me come into the room. We laugh so hard we cry as we share our sick and silly behaviors. We smile until our faces glow with joy and pride for each other as we share our progress. I see more honest smiles than I've seen for a long time. Slowly, my hope returns.

God, thank you for the smiles of others and the hope they can offer me.

REFLECT | *I can offer my smile and a lit-up face as a symbol of hope to others.*

Day 100 Living in My Feelings

READ | Job 30:15
Terrors overwhelm me; my dignity is driven away as by the wind, my safety vanishes like a cloud.

Turning my back on food means that I feel my emotions in their full intensity. Some days it seems as if I'm living in my feelings, and they chase all logic out the back door of my mind. Then I am left alone with those negative feelings and they threaten to thrash me. As one of my friends put it, "My head is like a dangerous neighborhood. I'm afraid to go in there without someone else."

I'm learning to take others with me into that dangerous neighborhood of my mind. I call friends and share my feelings, thus exposing my feelings to reality. I journal about those feelings and sort out which ones are true. Facing that truth helps me welcome my logic back into my head, and that can be a calming influence on my feelings.

Thank you for giving me feelings, but help me to process them in a healthy way.

REFLECT | *Feelings can help me, but I need to keep them in touch with reality.*

Day 101 More Will Be Revealed

READ | Job 31:33–34

If I have concealed my sin as men do, by hiding my guilt in my heart because I so feared the crowd . . .

I have concealed some of my sin so well that I don't even know what it is. I think I've forgiven people when I haven't. I think I've been generous when I haven't.

God reveals more to me as I surrender more of myself. As he sees that I am ready, he shows me how I've wounded a person's heart, how I've obsessed about money, and how I've ignored difficult people.

I can accept these things better as I quit beating myself up so much. As I shower grace on myself, he is free to show me what I am often like and to give me his overflowing, healing grace.

I yield myself to you, God,
to show me how I need to grow.

REFLECT | *I'm not the person I used to be, and I'm not the person God is helping me become.*

Day 102 Self-Obsession

READ | Job 32:2

But Elihu . . . became very angry with Job for justifying himself rather than God.

Job's accusers tried to find something wrong with Job, but could fault him for only one thing: he justified himself rather than God.

Like Job, I explain my actions until I become obsessed with myself. When accused, I defend myself with elaborate reasons. I have a high-toned excuse for each of my faults. I have crafty ways of designing conversations that make me look good and subtle ways of praising my own efforts. I constantly ask myself, "Is anyone looking at me?" "Did I say the right thing?" "Am I getting as much done as I should?" "Am I truly happy?" "Will I ever make it in life?"

Centering my life on God and learning how to eat sensibly helps me address my inner issues, but it also frees me from the need to focus on myself. That helps me reach out to others, and that in turn, frees me from being hung up on myself.

God, help me catch myself in my moments of habitual
self-obsession and turn my thoughts outward.

REFLECT | *I can be genuinely interested in others when I quit being preoccupied with myself.*

Day 103 Breaking the Isolation

READ | Job 32:20
I must speak and find relief; I must open my lips and reply.

Talking to people who also struggle with out-of-control ways of eating is important, because I've spent so much time in isolation that I've developed some dark behaviors that need to come out to the light. Finally, I can speak openly and honestly with a small group of people who share my struggles. I can share some of my darkest feelings and not feel judged.

Yet I want to be careful not to speak in personal conversations so honestly that it's difficult for others to tolerate.

It's easy to confuse other gatherings with support groups in which saying brutally honest things is appropriate, but I'm learning to distinguish appropriate settings from inappropriate ones.

In appropriate settings, the relief comes because there are others like me who make me feel loved and accepted—finally.

God, help me share things that will help me on my journey.

REFLECT | *I can and should share freely in appropriate settings.*

Day 104 Listening for God to Speak

READ | Job 33:14

For God does speak—now one way, now another—though man may not perceive it.

The voices of my old self are fading: Make yourself better by . . . fix that person by . . . stay in control by. . . . As they fade, I hear God speak more clearly.

God speaks to me through Scripture. He speaks through books and magazines that apply scriptural principles. He speaks through people in my support group. Sometimes he speaks through the nonsense, comfort, and confrontation of my friends. He speaks through sermons—especially the ones that I think I don't need. He can even speak through the beauty of my surroundings and the patches of dying grass.

I try to listen.

Thank you for the varied ways you guide me, God.

REFLECT | *I can listen for God's unlikely ways of speaking to me.*

Day 105 Second-Guessing God

READ | Job 36:26

How great is God—beyond our understanding!

With my over-analytical, private-detective mentality, I trust only what I understand. I've tried to figure out God, but not everything that happens seems to make sense. Every time I second-guess what God is up to, I'm wrong. He has given me things I don't think I want and withheld things I have begged for. This used to ignite a steady, burning bitterness in me.

I've decided to stop trying to understand God. This means that I quit peering over his shoulder to try to read the control panel. I sit back, shut my eyes, and try to enjoy the ride.

Why did I wait so long to do this?

God, I surrender to you my need to understand
everything that happens to me.

REFLECT | *I don't have to understand the journey, I just have to continue it.*

Day 106 Sleepless Anger

READ | Psalm 4:4

In your anger do not sin; when you are on your beds, search your hearts and be silent.

Some of my struggles do not surface during the day. I used to wake up at night and lie in bed letting anger and resentment take hold of me and thrash me around for hours as I tossed and turned. I rehearsed why I wasn't at fault and what I could have said to so-and-so. I lost a lot of sleep.

Now I recognize this as buried anger that needs to be faced. I can search my heart and discover what defects of character are in operation. Then I surrender them one by one. Out of these broken moments often comes a fierce determination to do what I can about myself and a peace to leave everyone else alone.

Help me work through the anger that keeps me awake.

REFLECT | *The thoughts that are hidden to me in daylight become apparent in the silence of night.*

Day 107 Daily Graces

READ | Psalm 5:3
In the morning, O LORD, you hear my voice; in the morning I lay my requests before you and wait in expectation.

As I first awaken in the morning, I invite God into my life that day. Before I sit up and my feet grope for my shoes, I ask God to help me by his grace. Before breakfast, I look at my menu for the day and commit myself to what I will and won't eat that day. A party tonight? Tough; I'll enjoy the people at the party instead of the goodies.

Throughout the day, I abide by my new ways of thinking and doing. I enjoy this new tendency to let go of the food, the anger, and the fear I once needed so badly. At night, I thank God for one more day of blessing.

Is this a dry ritual for me? No, these are moments of empowerment and even excitement between God and me.

God, please help me continue using all the tools you
have given me for the journey.

REFLECT | *I commit my life to God every day, one day at a
time.*

Day 108 Achievement Hunger

READ | Psalm 13:2

How long must I wrestle with my thoughts and every day have sorrow in my heart? How long will my enemy triumph over me?

When will my disordered eating evaporate? When will
I get beyond it? I don't like the answer: this is a lifelong
process. That high-achieving, perfectionistic part of myself
wants to get this job done, so I can move on to other
things. Yet when I least expect it, the drivenness becomes
strong and I would travel land and sea for a chocolate chip
cookie—now!

The battle continues, but so does my progress. I keep
practicing the tools of praying, calling friends, and trusting
God one more day. Progress is not measured by my achievements, but in the way I keep turning myself over to God
again and again.

I give up my need to "lick this thing" and offer you the
pieces of the puzzle, God.

REFLECT | *I feed my self-esteem with God's acceptance of me,
not with my so-called ability to take charge of my eating.*

Day 109 Practicing God's Presence

READ | Psalm 16:8
I have set the LORD always before me. Because he is at my right hand, I will not be shaken.

Before I begin each event of my day, I invite God to take part in it with me. I understand that God is present everywhere, but I go through this formality because I am learning to practice the presence of God, to maintain conscious contact with him.

I want to be more aware of God's presence, not so he can be my watchdog, but because I'm getting to know him better. I know that God is the person who loves me no matter what. With my still-flagging self-esteem, I can't seem to get enough of this unconditional acceptance.

I also practice God's presence because it gives me a window to serenity. It helps me see more quickly that nothing needs to rattle me into panicking, overeating, or thinking negatively.

Thank you that you are always with me,
God; help me to desire a greater awareness
of your presence.

REFLECT | *I flourish in God's presence as if I were a plant and God were the sun.*

Day 110 Pursuing My Dreams

READ | Psalm 20:4
May he give you the desire of your heart and make all your plans succeed.

I've pulled back from pursuing my dreams because I haven't believed in myself and I haven't thought that God believed in me, either. I didn't see myself as a capable person.

Now I'm learning that God has all kinds of interesting purposes for me and that he is working in me. I don't have to be shy, lazy, or withdrawn; he supplies me with the motivation and initiative I lack. I used to think I was useless, but I am not. Now, as a broken vessel for God, I am even more useful because I'm surrendering my will and I'm listening for God's direction. I am giving him my dreams, too, and asking him to show me if they are his will after all. Sometimes I don't sense his direction until I get out there and give it a try. Then I watch him open or shut doors, and his direction becomes clear to me.

God, help me know your will
about my dreams for the future.

REFLECT | *Since God believes in me enough to use me, I can pursue my dreams and see what happens.*

Day 111 Fear of Abandonment

READ | Psalm 22:11
Do not be far from me, for trouble is near and there is no one to help.

One of my greatest fears is that I will be abandoned. I have been afraid that a time will come when there will be no one to help me. It may happen because I alienate so many people or because I'm not interesting enough to love. Will I survive? Will I be alone in this world?

I see now that this fear of abandonment has tainted my actions. It has made me a people pleaser—so concerned about doing and being for others that I have no idea of what I'm really like and what I want.

As I'm learning who I am to God and sense my purpose here on earth, I feel more secure. That carries me through moments in which it seems that no one comes to help.

God, help me surrender my great fear
of abandonment to you.

R E F L E C T | *Abandonment itself can be endured; the fear of it makes me live in panic.*

Day 112 Me and My Enemy

R E A D | Psalm 23:5
You prepare a table before me in the presence of my enemies. You anoint my head with oil; my cup overflows.

This familiar verse pictures me seated with people who don't like me, yet I'm being honored with an anointing of God right in front of them! How different this picture is from the moments I've been shamed in front of others.

The spiritual enemy of God must be angry to see that I'm facing my eating problems. He is seated at the table, and he is frustrated that I refuse to wallow in negative thinking, that I actually try to solve problems without eating, and that I find life beyond food.

When I picture this scene I can see that I belong on the side of the table opposite the spiritual enemy behind my misguided eating. I am detached from it. I now have a new, separate identity.

God, thank you for blessing me in the presence of my
spiritual enemy.

REFLECT | *Facing up to problems means facing the clash of
powerful forces.*

Day 113 Traps from the Past

READ | Psalm 25:15
*My eyes are ever on the LORD, for only he will release my feet from
the snare.*

I would like to overlook the snares that entice me, such
as snacking while I fix meals, overdosing on diet drinks,
and resorting to liquid diets. As God shows me that these
behaviors are paths to destruction and not to wholeness,
they must go. My refusal to part with them tells me that I
am still holding out.

Yet my goal is to completely dethrone overeating and
dieting. I don't want those small behaviors to haunt me
or remind me of my former great devotion to disordered
living. If I let them, they can beat and bludgeon me and
convince me I have made no progress. These former
behaviors must go.

Please give me the determination to fully surrender
every part of my eating disorder to you, God.

REFLECT | *I can be willing, if not yet able, to surrender the
smallest of my unhealthy tendencies.*

Day 114 Brokenness Counts

R E A D | Psalm 34:18
The LORD is close to the brokenhearted and saves those who are crushed in spirit.

As long as I was self-assured and carefully restrained, I wasn't open to God. Now that I am desperate, broken, and crushed, I am eager for God to work in me.

The more I admit my neediness, the more needy I realize I am. The more I admit my faults, the less I'm surprised by them. The more I realize how crushed my spirit is, the more I find I'm useful to God.

My brokenness affects my body; many parts of it don't function well. My will seems almost gone, because it was my willfulness that kept me imprisoned. And my spirit is submitted to new practices of meditation and solitude.

Yet brokenness brings me to empowerment, I couldn't be empowered until I let go of the controls and gave them to God.

God, I surrender more and more of those crushed
places to you.

R E F L E C T | *Brokenness brings empowerment, not shame.*

Day 115 My Friend's Betrayal

R E A D | Psalm 41:9
Even my close friend, whom I trusted, he who shared my bread, has lifted up his heel against me.

My "close friend" not only shared my bread with me—my close friend *was* bread. It lifted its heel against me just as I trusted it to soothe my problems and give me confidence. Instead, it hid my problems in shadows and shriveled my confidence.

I tried to limit the drivenness of this friend, but diets stopped working. Starving myself was too scary an option. There was no talking sanity to this friend.

I am giving up bread as a close friend. I see the inappropriateness of trusting it when I can find safe people to trust. I can trust God as I learn to make conscious contact with him. As he changes me, I can even trust myself. I no longer feel the sting of bread's betrayal.

Please flood into my life, God,
and walk and talk with me so I won't miss
my close friend so much.

REFLECT | *Dethroning my eating behavior as a close friend leaves room for friendships with God and with healthy people.*

Day 116 God Honors Tears

READ | Psalm 56:8
Record my lament; list my tears on your scroll—are they not in your record?

In my anger, I've accused God of not caring that I'm hurting; but I know this is wrong. My tears are important to him; he honors them by recording each one. I know that I am loved and cared for.

Because I know this, I can cry without shame in front of my spiritual director and my support group. They honor my tears as God does. They understand that I must first grieve over my behavior before it can be changed.

Crying those tears of rigorous honesty cleanses me and releases me to make wise decisions.

Thank you for regarding my tears with respect, God.
Help me respect them, too.

REFLECT | *Tears of rigorous honesty deserve respect.*

Day 117 Resting in God

READ | Psalm 62:1
My soul finds rest in God alone; my salvation comes from him.

It's a new thought to rest in God. I thought God wanted me to work all the time and avoid fun and relaxation. I'm learning that God doesn't say that; my depleted self-esteem tells me to feel better about myself by working all the time.

I learn to rest in God as I quit hurrying through my day to do, do, do. I stop, listen, and enjoy others. I take walks and enjoy the beauty around me. I serve because I hear a gentle nudge from God, not because no one else will do it. I don't have to please anyone but God, and when I do, others will be more pleased in the long run.

God, plant your rest in my heart
and let it color my face and mannerisms.

REFLECT | *If I learn how to be with God, I will eventually do what I am supposed to do.*

√ Day 118 Unanswered Prayers

R E A D | Psalm 66:20
Praise be to God, who has not rejected my prayer or withheld his love from me!

I have prayed many frantic and well thought-out prayers that don't seem to have been answered. In those moments, I felt rejected and unloved, and that reinforced my suspicion that God was asleep or he didn't like me or I wasn't good enough.

As I set aside my I-want-it-now attitudes, I see that not having an immediate answer to my prayer doesn't mean that God has rejected me. He may answer my prayer with a "yes" or a "no" or a "wait." The answer is "yes" only if this is the right thing for me at exactly the right time.

I am no longer so afraid that God is rejecting me. Even when I suspect that he has not heard my prayer, I know that he has.

Help me to trust you, God, to answer my prayers
for my ultimate benefit.

R E F L E C T | *Unanswered prayer is simply an answer that I don't yet understand.*

√ Day 119 Becoming Whole

R E A D | Psalm 90:8
You have set our iniquities before you, our secret sins in the light of your presence.

I used to pretend my unbalanced eating didn't exist because I hid it so well and no one said anything about it. When I began to feel troubled in the midst of trying to be terribly nice, I felt needy for food. It was as if I would say, "Excuse me for a moment, God. I'll be right back. I have to do something."

Common sense tells me to keep hiding my secret sins, but I'm learning that it works better to pour out my feelings to God immediately. With that honesty, I no longer feel like two different people living in two different worlds. These two worlds have met each other, and I am facing myself and learning to live with myself. I am *one* person—a person who isn't terribly nice, but who also isn't so disordered. I'm simply healing and finding a new wholeness.

Thank you that you love me, God, even though you see my agitated side so clearly.

REFLECT | *Admitting that I have an eating problem releases me from wearing two different masks.*

Day 120 Protected in My Shelter

READ | Psalm 91:1
He who dwells in the shelter of the Most High will rest in the shadow of the Almighty.

I no longer need to protect myself by withdrawing or lashing out in anger. I don't even need the protection of unbalanced eating. I have found protection by renewing my God-given choices and boundaries.

I can choose to forgive instead of feeling hurt by others' comments. I can choose to overlook others' faults instead of magnifying them. I can choose to speak up calmly to those who violate my boundaries of time, privacy, or familiarity instead of resenting those people.

Healthy choices and boundaries are part of the God-given shelter that I am born with, and I will reclaim them as best I can.

> Show me, God, healthy boundaries,
> and help me to live within them.

R E F L E C T | *No one will respect my boundaries unless I respect them myself.*

Day 121 Unfathomable Forgiveness

R E A D | Psalm 103:2–3

*Praise the L*ORD *. . . who forgives all your sins and heals all your diseases.*

If God forgives me, then I can forgive me. God chooses to forget my past misbehaviors and the destructive things I've said about and felt toward people, and I need to do the same thing. Beating myself up doesn't make me a better person; it makes me a bitter person.

This overflowing forgiveness is empowering. It means that I can make amends to someone with no fear of how they will react. It means that I can stand up before others with confidence—not because I want to impress them, but because God has forgiven me. It means that I have no illusions about how wonderful I am, but that I rest in the thought that I am dearly loved by God. It means that when I fail, I can start over.

> God, help me rest in your forgiveness.

R E F L E C T | *God is more merciful to me than I can ever be.*

Day 122 Switching Snares

READ | Psalm 106:36
They worshiped their idols, which became a snare to them.

As an admitted worshiper of food and thinness, I'm a prime candidate to worship something else as I give up my old ways of eating. New obsessions appear in front of me as silvery idols to snare me. I may become overly preoccupied with fun and entertainment, work and productivity, even self-improvement itself.

I can surrender each idol and turn it over to God. If I don't, an innocent substance can become a snare for me because of my inner neediness. I must, once again, let God do for me what I cannot do for myself.

God, help me see these silvery idols as the traps they really are, and surrender them.

REFLECT | *Whatever I spend too much time thinking about is my idol.*

Day 123 Unlimited Love

READ | Psalm 107:21
Let them give thanks to the LORD for his unfailing love and his wonderful deeds for men.

No matter how I look or how negatively my body compares to those of the beautiful people in magazine ads, God loves me. No matter how I feel—angry, frustrated, or withdrawn—God loves me.

I often have feelings that I'm failing because I'm not showing results quickly enough. I sometimes think that my friends are thinking the same things about me. But I can trust God not to think less of me because I'm not improving fast enough. He is the one who will not desert me when I blow it one afternoon or morning. He is the one who will scoop me up out of my heap of exhaustion and help me walk again.

God's love will never fail me. I can't do anything to make him stop loving me.

Thank you that you never reject me, ignore me, or harshly scold me, God.

REFLECT | *God's love is not limited by my flaws.*

Day 124 Savoring Scripture

READ | Psalm 119:15
I meditate on your precepts and consider your ways.

Some days I gobble down Scripture verses about as fast as I used to eat M&Ms. I feel no enjoyment, just the need to get through the bag—or the Bible passage.

The idea of digesting and absorbing Scripture is new. I can read a few verses, shut my eyes to block out distractions, and consider what these verses mean in my life. If God were going to speak to me through this passage, what would he say?

I can't say for sure that it's God speaking, but when I do this, great ideas come to me: a small thing I need to start doing, something I need to say to someone, or someone I haven't called. I can write down these ideas and consider how to put them into action.

Thank you for the powerful ideas that come from
meditating on your Word.

REFLECT | *Meditation is to Scripture as savoring is to
food.*

Day 125 Becoming Still

READ | Psalm 131:2
*But I have stilled and quieted my soul; like a weaned child with its
mother, like a weaned child is my soul within me.*

In times of panic, I have at least three choices:
- I can assume the worst will happen and fly
  into a frenzy.
- I can stuff myself with food or exercise myself into a
  stupor.
- I can use my tools and process my fears.

My soul can be stilled and quieted without being force-
fed. This shift from panic to serenity is not instantaneous.
As I journal, call a friend, or go to a meeting, my self-talk
gets healthier and I cast aside my negative thinking. Soon I
am at peace with myself and my world.

Help me to learn the skill of quieting my soul
and build it into a habit.

REFLECT | *I have the capacity to still and quiet my soul, if
I will.*

Day 126 Wonderful Body Shapes

READ | Psalm 139:14–16

I praise you because I am fearfully and wonderfully made; your works are wonderful. . . . When I was woven together in the depths of the earth, your eyes saw my unformed body.

I have felt ashamed of my body because it isn't shaped the way my culture says it should be. I have sized myself up and decided that no matter what size I am, it is wrong. I dread looking in the mirror. Saying my body is wonderful seems overstated and, quite truthfully, a lie.

It takes a while to agree with God that my body is wonderfully made. God created all types of body shapes and sizes, not preferring one over the other. A pear-shaped body is as wonderful to him as any other. My culture's preference for certain sizes and shapes over others is arbitrary. My culture's prejudice in labeling certain body shapes and sizes as misshapen and ugly violates God's truth. All body shapes and sizes are wonderfully made because of who made them.

God, please take away my self-loathing for my body
and replace it with self-respect.

REFLECT | *All body shapes and sizes are the work of God's creation.*

Day 127 Grandiosity Unveiled

READ | Proverbs 3:7

Do not be wise in your own eyes.

The word *grandiosity* means being wise in one's own eyes. I've been grandiose when I've known the answer to every dilemma, when I've thought I could solve my weight problem in a minute—if I wanted to, when I've thought I could solve everyone's problems if they did things my way.

The antidote to my grandiosity is understanding the severe limitations of being human. My compulsive eating behaviors made my limitations obvious and began shattering my grandiosity. The more I understand just how much my eating behaviors thwarted me, the more humble I feel. I am ready to acknowledge the frailness and fragility of my own humanness and surrender to the unlimited wisdom of God.

> God, keep showing me the truth about
> my many grandiose ideas about life.

REFLECT | *Getting in touch with my grandiosity shows me my need for God.*

Day 128 Sexuality

READ | Proverbs 5:18
May your fountain be blessed, and may you rejoice in the wife of your youth.

My all-or-nothing, black-and-white thinking led me to believe these extreme myths about sexuality:

Prudery—I didn't deserve to understand or enjoy my sexuality.

Promiscuity—I needed to express my sexuality casually to get people to notice or love me.

As I choose not to think in extremes, I can accept that God created me to be a sexual person and I can channel this gift appropriately. I can enjoy an appropriate sexual relationship. I can take pleasure in dressing according to my gender without calling attention to myself.

Help me to not run away from my sexuality
or to overindulge it, God. Help me see it as you see it.

REFLECT | *Sexuality is God's gift, and I can enjoy it as God designed it.*

Day 129 The Fear of God

READ | Proverbs 9:10
The fear of the LORD is the beginning of wisdom, and knowledge of the Holy One is understanding.

People who loathe themselves as much as I have can easily misunderstand the "fear of the Lord." The fear of the Lord is not, as some would suppose, terror of a whimsical, powerful tyrant who wields thunderbolts for the fun of it. But it is also not simple awe and reverence.

It is a sensible, healthy, respectful fear for a powerful being. He is not a childish dictator, but he is also not a best pal or a permissive parent. I can barely understand God because he encompasses dimensions of justice and mercy that reach beyond human understanding. He is God, and to fear him is not to be terrified, but to respect and treat him as an all-powerful supreme being.

God, I want to acknowledge and fear you
as the powerful being you are without being so fearful of
you that I can't relate to you.

REFLECT | *Wisdom involves understanding that God is the*
Holy One.

Day 130 The Pretending Game

READ | Proverbs 12:9
Better to be a nobody and yet have a servant than pretend to be some-
body and have no food.

Pretending is exhausting. It robs me of my inner
resources and puts me on guard at all times. I can't relax
with others, with myself, or even with God.

Sometimes I pretend to be a more confident, capable
person. At other times I pretend to be a troublemaker
because there's something in me that likes to create chaos.
At still other times I pretend to be quiet and withdrawn,
because I'm scared of the confident people around me. As
long as I wear these masks, I have to keep up the facade and
not bare myself to anyone.

As I admit that I am an overeater, I'm free to be just
me—no more, no less. I don't need everyone to like me,
because the love of God and the love of friends are calming
my need for acceptance.

Thank you for loving me for who I am.
Help me to trust that and to shed my masks.

REFLECT | *God and others accept me as I am, and I can do*
that, too.

101

Day 131 The D Word: Discipline

R E A D | Proverbs 13:18
He who ignores discipline comes to poverty and shame, but whoever heeds correction is honored.

I don't like the word *disciplined* because it makes me think of the way I beat myself up and badger myself into doing the right thing. Then I react to my own harshness and want to overeat.

"It works if you work it" is a gentle way of saying that I can discipline myself. I do the footwork by using the tools God has given me. I need to talk with others about my journey, hearing their stories and sharing mine. I need to read the Bible and books on spirituality and wholeness in order to remind me of how I can grow. I need to find a wise mentor or spiritual director to partner with me in this journey. These tools correct my old thinking and renew my mind. They help me look at myself and surrender to God.

God, help me humble myself once again and take up
the tools I've put down.

R E F L E C T | *Discipline is not beating myself up. It's using my tools.*

Day 132 Smart Answers

R E A D | Proverbs 15:1
A gentle answer turns away wrath, but a harsh word stirs up anger.

"When in doubt, leave it out" is one of my mottoes now. I've decided to give up my grandiose, know-it-all attitude. I don't have to air every observation, opinion, or accusation that comes ripping through my mind.

I'm giving up clever comebacks and put-downs. They make me feel guilty afterward. If I don't come up with them, I'm tempted later to turn the conversation over and over in my mind until I do think of one.

My gentle answer turns away my wrath as well as everyone else's. I feel better when I'm gentle. I don't need to use food to assuage my anger and guilt, and I feel generous toward others.

Thank you for the grace to pull back
when I feel the need to run over people
with my words.

REFLECT | *My gentle answer turns away my wrath.*

Day 133 Living in the Present

READ | Proverbs 15:15
All the days of the oppressed are wretched, but the cheerful heart has a continual feast.

A continual zero-calorie feast is the dream of every compulsive overeater and dieter. In its broadest sense, a continual feast is a day in which I enjoy each food that is brought before me.

As I find a new wholeness, I realize that a continual feast is much different. It is enjoying each moment as it comes rather than worrying about the past and the future. I can continually feast in the present moment when I trust God that whatever happens will turn out for my benefit.

The people and events of today are set before me, and I can choose to enjoy them, ignore them, or complain about them. This is my choice.

> God, help me experience each moment
> as it comes and enjoy each moment as
> much as possible.

REFLECT | *Life can be something like a continual feast if I allow it to be.*

Day 134 Separate Purposes

READ | Proverbs 15:17
Better a meal of vegetables where there is love than a fattened calf with hatred.

Meals were meant to be celebrations where people share love. To provide a meal for another person is a concrete way to show love. But I have been so focused on whether or not the food is tasty or there's enough of it that I have overlooked the people sitting at the table with me.

Instead, I'm learning to let God address my need for love so I am free to reach out to others at mealtime. I don't have to be so obsessed with what is being served and its calorie count, but instead I can put my fork down and listen to others tell stories and share their ideas. Mealtime is no longer a place where I ignore people.

And when it's my turn to provide a meal and hospitality for others, I can actually think about serving other people instead of being fixated on how good or how bad the food is.

O God, help me to use food and mealtimes to welcome others into my life.

REFLECT | *Mealtime can be a way to show love to others.*

Day 135 When Self-Talk Goes Wild

READ | Proverbs 15:28
The heart of the righteous weighs its answers. . . .

My negative self-talk is like traffic in my head that drowns out God's promptings. I'm learning to weigh how I answer my self-talk:

- I don't have to expect the worst. I will wait and see what happens.
- I don't have to feel persecuted. No one is out to get me. I will give the other person the benefit of the doubt.
- I don't have to expect myself and others to be perfect. There is no such thing as an all-caring parent, best friend, or spouse.

God knows my heart, and he is teaching me to calm and comfort myself. He asks me to rest in his presence and helps me to quiet my anxiety.

God, renew my mind by helping me correct my negative self-talk.

REFLECT | *I can answer my negative self-talk with wisdom.*

Day 136 Flexibility

READ | Proverbs 16:9

In his heart a man plans his course, but the LORD determines his steps.

I have coped with life and with weight gains by using rigid attempts to control myself. I planned and planned and planned my food, my diets, and my life events only to find that no plan considered all the contingencies. No eating plan had my name on it.

As I give up my out-of-control eating behaviors, I also give up rigidity and excessive controlling. I let things happen, and I ask God to help me cope with them. Every time I panic, I feel the urge to control, but I give it up again.

All plans are tentative now. I understand that God determines my steps so I make my needs known, plan a possible course, and watch with anticipation to see what will happen.

Help me surrender to you, God, my need to control.

REFLECT | *Flexibility begins with giving God my plans.*

Day 137 When Logic Fails

READ | Proverbs 16:25

There is a way that seems right to a man, but in the end it leads to death.

Many things that seemed logical and practical to me no longer seem so. My out-of-the-ordinary eating behaviors seemed to solve my problems of staying thin, getting rid of anger, and killing off my appetite, but they backfired. My body deteriorated, and my life became unmanageable.

My logic failed me at other times, too. I thought beating myself up would motivate me to work harder in life, but it made me feel worthless. Pretending to feel fine worked only until the next crisis occurred.

Now when something seems logical to me, I run it past God in prayer and I check it out with others. I understand that what seems right to me may turn out to be wrong, and when it is, I try to learn from it.

Help me set aside logical conclusions and wait for more information and insight from you.

REFLECT | *Just because something seems logical or practical doesn't make it right.*

Day 138 Confidentiality

READ | Proverbs 17:9

He who covers over an offense promotes love, but whoever repeats the matter separates close friends.

Sometimes when others tell me things they've done, I get on my high horse and say, "At least I've never done that!" Then the next day I come within inches of doing something similar, so I end up confessing my judgmental attitude to God.

Slowly I'm learning not to judge people or talk about their mistakes. They are not terrible; they are like me. They're bound up in a powerful inner struggle, and they need my love and acceptance.

Besides, when I gloat about others' defects, it distracts me from my own struggling attempts to do whatever it takes to surrender my compulsive behaviors. I don't need additional distractions, so I need to forego gossip and obsessive judgment of others for my own good as well.

God, thank you that others trust me to love
them the way you love me. Help me to keep
attempting to do that.

REFLECT | *Confidentiality means I don't expose others' secrets to outsiders or to my own prideful judgments.*

√Day 139 Taking Life Less Seriously

READ | Proverbs 17:22
A cheerful heart is good medicine, but a crushed spirit dries up the bones.

Recovering from an eating problem is not a gloom-and-doom experience. In my support group I'm learning to laugh about how paranoid and panicky I am about my eating. At first, all that laughter in those groups seems strange, but the laughter is part of surrendering to God and admitting powerlessness. It's how compulsive people identify with one another and accept one another.

Now that I feel more accepted, I don't worry so much about how I look when I make mistakes. I can even laugh at old pictures of myself. I'm not so self-conscious about what I draw, write, cook, or build. So what if it's not perfect? Neither am I.

Laughing at my mistakes tells me and others that I have let go of the controls. What a relief!

Thank you, God, for helping me take myself less
seriously and your interest in me very seriously.

REFLECT | *I take myself too seriously when I'm my only hope.*

Day 140 Balanced Thinking

READ | Proverbs 17:24
*A discerning man keeps wisdom in view, but a fool's eyes wander to
the ends of the earth.*

It's possible to wander off into a completely spiritual
or psychological approach to wholeness without respect for
the way my body works and metabolizes food. I can fool
myself into thinking:

- If I work through all my issues, it won't matter if I
  eat a lot of high-fat foods.
- If I pray every day, it won't matter if I never exercise
  (or exercise too much).

Respect for the workings of my body means that I abide
by accepted general principles of exercise and nutrition
and I put them into practice without becoming obsessed by
them. When I ignore them, I'm in the same kind of denial I
was in before my eating problems came to control me. I'm
buying into magical thinking because I don't want to do
necessary, but difficult, things.

God, show me how I can use exercise and nutrition
properly to energize and care for my body
without beating myself up.

REFLECT | *If I don't want to be rigorously honest, I need to
ask myself why.*

Day 141 Listening Well

READ | Proverbs 18:13
He who answers before listening—that is his folly and his shame.

The no-crosstalk rule used in my support group (for more explanation, see glossary) works well in relationships, too. When I don't allow myself to interrupt, others have a chance to say what they feel. As they wander around in their thoughts, they eventually spit out what they think. And I'm glad I gave them time, because now I know them better.

I don't rush in anymore—to rescue with answers, to defend my position, or to stop the flow of tears. I also try not to analyze or talk back in my thoughts. I try to give all my attention to listening. I allow people to be themselves, and I respect them with my silence.

God, help me value others the way you do—
by listening to them with no worry of how much they do
or don't make sense.

REFLECT | *When I silence the traffic in my head, I hear more of what others are trying to say.*

Day 142 To Be Unoffendable

READ | Proverbs 19:11
A man's wisdom gives him patience; it is to his glory to overlook an offense.

When someone offends me, it's no longer a major event in my life. I don't have to dwell on it or analyze how much they meant to insult me. I don't have to rehearse how I can confront them. I'm learning to give up the offense and overlook it. Even if it was intended, I can temper my conclusions with mercy.

People who overlook offenses are easy to be with. They don't misunderstand me and misinterpret what I say as a negative comment about them. I don't have to go back and say, "I hope you didn't think I meant. . . ." At first I mistook this positive nature as naivety and weakness, but now I see it as serenity and strength. I want the same thing for myself.

Help me, God, to give grace to others
as you give grace to me.

REFLECT | *Whether I choose to be offended says more about me than about the other person.*

Day 143 Drawing Others Out

READ | Proverbs 20:5
The purposes of a man's heart are deep waters, but a man of understanding draws them out.

I'm learning to ask more questions and give fewer answers. I see my defects of character so clearly now that I know I'm not a fountain of wisdom anymore.

Now I have a lot more faith in people's ability to understand themselves. They sit in support groups and talk through issues that have puzzled them for years—with no help from me!

When people ask my advice or my opinion, I'm more likely to draw them out now. I pose questions. I reflect their feelings back to them. Then I ask that tough question: What do you think God wants you to do?

Help me draw others out
instead of spouting off what I know.

REFLECT | *I help others more by helping them help themselves.*

✓Day 144 Moody Blues

READ | Proverbs 21:9
Better to live on a corner of the roof than share a house with a quarrelsome wife.

When I felt quarrelsome, even I didn't like living with me. The feeling of grouchiness loomed over me—and everyone else—like a threatening cloud from which no one could escape.

Admitting to myself that I have a problem with grouchiness gives me the desire to surrender it. Frequently I journal about it or call someone to avoid spreading it within my family and co-workers. Facing the problem also helps me get at the root of my grouchy feelings of fear, anger, or self-pity so I can surrender them.

I see now why someone would rather sit on a roof in all kinds of weather rather than be around me when I'm brooding. As my moody moments become less frequent, others want to be around me more.

God, please rid me of the grouchiness that seems to
stick to me like wet clothing.

REFLECT | *I can choose whether I will nurse my moodiness or confront it.*

Day 145 Cravings

READ | Proverbs 21:25–26
The sluggard's craving will be the death of him, because his hands refuse to work. All day long he craves for more. . . .

I have been so focused on eating and not eating that I have ignored my health, my goals, and my dreams. I have felt guilty for giving in to my cravings and I've told myself I'd never amount to anything anyway, so why try? I've daydreamed and fantasized about food, so I've sacrificed the good things I wanted to do. There wasn't time to read a book or see a friend—I had to find a store and buy some ice cream.

Now that I'm surrendering these cravings to God, I have time for life. I make appointments with the doctor when I need to; I build relationships with those I previously envied for their smaller size; I need less time to snack so I have more time to enjoy gardening or playing volleyball.

God, help me see facets of life open to me as I shut the door on my cravings.

REFLECT | *As I get rid of my cravings, I can "get a life."*

Day 146 Excuses

READ | Proverbs 22:13
The sluggard says, "There is a lion outside!" or, "I will be murdered in the streets!"

Just as a lazy person makes excuses for not going to work, I have my reasons for my strange relationship with food.

- I am overweight because I'm big-boned.
- Dieting gives me control.
- It's good for me to snack or skip meals.

As I face the truth about myself in light of God's abundant love for me, I can admit the truth: I am obsessed with food; I am obsessed with thinness.

There is no lion outside. The lion is within me, driving me to be out of balance. As I relinquish my excuses and admit the truth about myself, I am opening the doors of my house and rushing outside. With God's help, I have hope and courage to tame the lion within me.

God, help me admit the excuses and cover-ups I've been using for my eating behaviors.

REFLECT | *My imbalanced eating behaviors come from within, not from without.*

Day 147 Enthusiasm

READ | Proverbs 23:18
There is surely a future hope for you, and your hope will not be cut off.

Will anything ever get better? Will I ever amount to anything? What can be expected from a compulsive person?

My fears about my future being "cut off" were normal for someone who buried their worries in eating. Nothing seemed to work. But now I'm surrendering myself to God, and that gives me hope because he has the power to change me.

To be hopeful feels good and presents the possibility of being enthusiastic once again. The word *enthusiasm* comes from the two Greek words *en* and *theos* meaning "God within." When I remain in the God who is within me, I have every reason to be filled with hope and anticipation about my future.

Thank you, God, for giving me a future and a hope.

REFLECT | *Enthusiasm is the child of hope.*

Day 148 Removing Obstacles

READ | Proverbs 25:16
If you find honey, eat just enough—too much of it, and you will vomit.

Some foods are like honey; they are fine as long as I don't have too much of them. When I start daydreaming about certain foods, I abstain from them. When I become obsessive about weighing myself, I ask someone to hide the scales for a month.

Rigorous honesty demands that I eliminate from my life the foods and eating behaviors that drive me. It's tempting to rationalize that they are not a problem, but the more I see the benefits of eating sensibly, the more quickly I identify those driven things and abstain from them.

I don't consider that I'm depriving myself, but that I'm focusing my energies on the best things: relationships, work, and knowledge of God's love.

Please help me, God, to recognize my driven behaviors and abstain from them.

REFLECT | *Committing my way of eating to God means listening to him about how it needs to be refined.*

Day 149 Others' Boundaries

R E A D | Proverbs 25:17
Seldom set foot in your neighbor's house—too much of you, and he will hate you.

Setting foot in my neighbor's house is fine as long as she wants it that way. She's prepared to talk for a while and give me refreshment if I need it. This is delightful, but I won't expect her to do it again tomorrow or the next day.

I'm learning to respect the boundaries of others. I don't dump my thoughts or feelings on people who aren't equipped to hear them. Even with close friends, I don't go on and on about myself.

When I involve other people in my progress toward wholeness, I respect their boundaries of time and privacy. I'm grateful for what they give me, and I don't demand more or feel disappointed when they aren't able to give more.

Thank you, God, for the people you've sent to love me, and help me treat them with respect.

R E F L E C T | *People find it easier to love me when I don't expect so much of them.*

Day 150 Confession Prospers

R E A D | Proverbs 28:13
He who conceals his sins does not prosper, but whoever confesses and renounces them finds mercy.

Concealing my eating problems was important. I felt that if people knew about them, they wouldn't like me.

Now I find that admitting the disgusting behaviors of my old ways of eating opens me to God's mercy. I share them with my group and hang my head, feeling as if no one will ever speak to me again. But I look up to find others nodding in agreement. What relief! Others know the truth about me and still accept me. Their attitude of pardon puts skin on God, so to speak, and I feel even more assured that I am forgiven.

These new attitudes of honesty and transparency prosper me. They allow me to be intimate in a healthy way, to quit trying to impress people, and to admit my mistakes with candor. I feel freer than I ever have to be the person God created me to be.

Thank you, God, for showing me that openness and humility lead to wholeness.

REFLECT | *Sharing my secrets in a safe environment helps me grow.*

Day 151 Obsessed with Thinness

READ | Proverbs 29:25
Fear of man will prove to be a snare, but whoever trusts in the LORD is kept safe.

Trying to please others is impossible, but I thought I was a Superperson, so I tried. When it didn't work, I ate. Then I found that no matter how much I tried this or that, there was no pleasing the cultural standard of thinness.

Nothing satisfies my culture except a pencil-thin and tummy-tucked body. Some movie stars use body doubles for distant shots; others use body doubles for close-up shots. Yet

I berate myself because my body will never conform to that perfect body image that even movie stars don't achieve.

That image is not worth achieving. It's safer to trust God to show me the goal weight that is best for me and to help me find the necessary tools to achieve it. Unlike our culture, God doesn't hold it against me if it takes me a while to do this.

> God, please keep me focused on becoming a whole
> person and help me avoid becoming obsessed
> with thinness.

R E F L E C T | *My goal is to return to a normal weight for my body—no more, no less.*

Day 152 Hooked on Productivity

R E A D | Ecclesiastes 4:8
There was no end to his toil, yet his eyes were not content with his wealth.

Work is generally a good thing unless it becomes compulsive. Alongside my disordered eating, I feel the urge to prove myself to the world. I do this by:

- being a compulsive volunteer, saying "yes" to whatever is asked of me, and making sure I do the best job that's ever been done for that task;
- finding my "career path" and hiking down that path faster and farther than anyone who has gone before me;
- hurrying my life away doing twenty things at once; and
- feeling good only when I accomplish many or all the things on my daily checklist.

I can surrender this, too, because it is no different from my eating problems in its frenzied attempt to fill my neediness.

> God, help me see the similarity between my
> eating problems and the other things in life
> that drive me.

REFLECT | *Compulsive working looks more respectable but is no less debilitating than disordered eating.*

Day 153 I Can Do It Myself!

READ | Ecclesiastes 4:9
Two are better than one, because they have a good return for their work.

Everything within me convinces me that I can beat my eating problems alone. I, the "lone ranger," have never needed anyone. Who says I need someone now? Why should I have to drive across town to a silly meeting full of people with problems of their own? What do those people know that I don't?

It's not what those people know, it's what they are. I need to be around them to see that I am one of many with an unhealthy relationship to food. I need to hear their stories to confirm within myself that I am not crazy. I need to share at the meeting so I can hear words come out of my own mouth about why I want to change. I need to hear others' words echo over the next few days as I face the tiger in myself.

I need those people, and they need me; God made it that way.

God, help me humble myself enough to reach out
to go to a meeting.

REFLECT | *Isolation is a symptom of pride and grandiosity;
reaching out is a sign of surrender.*

Day 154 Asking for Help

READ | Ecclesiastes 4:10
*If one falls down, his friend can help him up. But pity the man who
falls and has no one to help him up!*

Before friends can help me up, I have to notify them
that I've fallen down. Sometimes I have trouble with that.
Asking for help assumes that I am a valued person, and I'm
just beginning to believe that asking for help means I have
to trust someone, and I'm just beginning to trust others.

But at times I gather my courage and call a friend on
the telephone, and when I do, I am helped so much. I hear
my angry and hurt thoughts expressed aloud, and I release
them. I hear my eager and determined thoughts become
audible words, and I renew my courage to go on.

I hang up the telephone feeling as if I'm starting a new
day. I'm excited about what is to come.

Please give me courage to make a telephone call to a
friend when I need support.

REFLECT | *Friendship is not a luxury, but a necessity.*

Day 155 Accountability Works

R E A D | Ecclesiastes 4:12
Though one may be overpowered, two can defend themselves. A cord of three strands is not quickly broken.

When I make myself accountable to others, I wrap a strong protective cord around me. I can go back to my life knowing that I'm safely tethered to others, and that tether provides strength.

I, who lack willpower, am now empowered by my partnership with others. Knowing that they stand beside me in my efforts to surrender my compulsiveness, rage, and self-pity makes me stand taller. I don't give in so quickly because it's more than just me who's fighting this thing.

The intense look in their eyes and the serious set of their jaws tell me that I can depend on them to be strong when I am weak.

God, help me humble myself enough to make myself
accountable as often as I need to.

R E F L E C T | *Accountability empowers.*

Day 156 Risky Business

R E A D | Ecclesiastes 11:1
Cast your bread upon the waters, for after many days you will find it again.

It is risky, even absurd, to throw food away. But God tells me that if I risk enough to surrender my food to him, he will bring it back to me in my time of need. When it does come back it is in the form of spiritual bread. I am ready to receive it because I'm making more room in my life for it.

Faith is a risky business. I must believe enough in God's love to trust him to give me what I need, even though it looks as if I'm giving up exactly what I need.

But it is exciting. I give up food, and God sustains me. I give up the need to impress others, and God impresses them for me. I give up control, and God controls events better than I ever could.

God, help me move down this risky path of surrender.

REFLECT | *The path to wholeness is the wisest risk I can take and will yield the greatest returns.*

Day 157 From the Inside Out

READ | Song of Solomon 7:6
How beautiful you are and how pleasing, O love, with your delights!

No matter how many compliments I receive on my appearance, I can name many things wrong with it. My face is not clear enough, my hair looks scruffy, my hips—don't even talk about them.

The woman to whom today's verse was spoken may or may not have been a knockout beauty, but the love and positive flow between her lover and her created her beauty. This helps me see that my attitudes can make me more attractive.

For example, I am more attractive when I take it easy on myself. My face and gestures relax and a genuine smile lights up my face. I accept myself to the point that I enjoy working on my appearance. I understand that being attractive comes from inner peace as well as the peace I've made with the looks that the Creator God gave me.

God, help me become attractive from the inside out.

R E F L E C T | *My body becomes as attractive as my attitudes.*

Day 158 Life as a Problem Solver

R E A D | Isaiah 1:18
"Come now, let us reason together," says the LORD. "Though your sins are like scarlet, they shall be as white as snow; though they are red as crimson, they shall be like wool."

I used to say to food, "Let us escape together over problems." God says to me, "Let us reason together over solutions."

I want to be solution-oriented, too. For too long I have muddled over problems by blaming others and escaping in food. It feels different to solve a problem the way I tackle a jigsaw puzzle. I am learning to allay my initial panic and examine the problem from all sides. I commit myself to stay with it until I figure out the puzzle or find someone who can.

I praise you, God, the tackler of great problems.

R E F L E C T | *Maturity means working through problems.*

Day 159 Out of the Darkness

READ | Isaiah 9:2
The people walking in darkness have seen a great light; on those living in the land of the shadow of death a light has dawned.

Facing my eating problem is transforming me. My thinking and my way of life are different. I am changing from one who walks in the darkness of panic to one who walks in the light of serenity. I'm escaping from the "shadow of death" of the junk-food malnutrition and high blood pressure that could have robbed me of life. I may still struggle, but I am being freed. I'm emerging wounded yet wise, surrendered yet strong.

In Isaiah's day, the nation of Judah was losing its integrity and national strength, but God worked with Judah and turned the nation into an instrument for him. He is doing the same thing with me. He's done it before; I can trust him to keep doing it with me.

Thank you, God, that with you anything is possible.

REFLECT | *Wholeness can become a reality in my life.*

Day 160 The Drive to Feel Good

READ | Isaiah 25:8
The Sovereign Lord will wipe away the tears from all faces; he will remove the disgrace of his people from all the earth.

When I read words like those in the verse above, I want to shout, "When? When? When?!" I know that God won't wipe away sorrow until the next life, but I keep hoping for something sooner.

I have felt so driven to feel good that I've tried to use food to achieve it. I'm not good at sitting with my hurt and enduring it. I want to take the soft, easy way, not the long, difficult one.

I am learning that some things are more important than feeling good—serenity, treating others fairly, fulfilling God's purposes for me, and persevering even if it feels miserable. So I go along with this new approach and look forward to the feel-good days of the future.

> Please help me set aside the desire to feel
> good all the time and take up new desires
> for serenity and purpose.

REFLECT | *My goal is long-term contentment, not a quick fix.*

Day 161 Steady Serenity

READ | Isaiah 26:3
You will keep in perfect peace him whose mind is steadfast, because he trusts in you.

When I haven't been pleased with the circumstances and people in my life, I've tried to control them. For a while, I got what I wanted, but it forced me to be more controlling. The more I tried to manage my world, the more compulsive I became. What is repeated fad dieting but weight control gone mad?

Serenity is based on having a steady mind even when I cannot control anything around me. It is a renewed mind that rejects the myths of my culture that money, fame, or thinness will make me "good enough." It's a refocused

125

mind that doesn't chase after more and more things to try to be happy.

I can let go of control and let God direct things. I can agree with God that he has given me everything I need.

God, I trust you to take control.

REFLECT | *The more I trust God, the more I learn serenity.*

Day 162 Mixed Motives

READ | Isaiah 29:13

These people . . . honor me with their lips, but their hearts are far from me.

For years I've said the right words and done the right things, but with questionable motives. I've helped people because I didn't want to feel guilty or because I didn't want to upset them. All that guilt and maneuvering played into my eating problems, and I paid for each mixed motive with candy bars, French fries, and extra helpings at dinner.

It's important to sort out my motives. If I stop doing things just because I feel guilty, what will I stop doing? What encouraging words will I stop offering simply to get people to like me?

Not until I stop doing things with mixed motives can I unearth my positive motives. Then I can be free to be caring and kind from a full heart.

Help me to have a pure heart, God,
and to acknowledge when I don't.

REFLECT | *My goal is to speak and act as authentically as I am able.*

126

Day 163 Strength in Quietness

R E A D | Isaiah 30:15

In repentance and rest is your salvation, in quietness and trust is your strength.

Just as I'm learning to open up and talk, I'm learning to be quiet, too.

Sometimes I free myself of my frustration by sharing it with friends who are on a similar path, but at other times it's better to sit with it and be quiet. I've harped on it long enough, and I've learned all I can. Now it's time to wait because it's beyond my control and I can't change it by talking about it. Perhaps I will learn more from waiting on it than from talking about it.

This is not a gagged silence. It's a voluntary one in which I trust that something is going to occur if I simply leave things alone. As I turn it over to God, I release it and watch what happens.

God, help me simmer down and trust you.

R E F L E C T | *Being quiet cuts through the traffic in my mind and helps me listen to what God may be saying.*

Day 164 Beating Myself Up

R E A D | Isaiah 43:18

Forget the former things; do not dwell on the past.

Part of what has fed my compulsion has been beating myself up for the things I've done wrong in the past. I've dwelt on the many unkind things I've thought and said and the unwise decisions I've made.

God didn't beat up the nation of Judah, heaping blame and shame on them, although they had been faithless. He urged them not to dwell on their past failures and challenged them to move ahead.

He follows the same path with me, and this helps me see the futility of beating myself up. Yes, I've made mistakes. But I seek forgiveness, make amends when possible, and go on. I believe that God can change me into a different person.

God, give me the strength to forgive myself and others and move on.

REFLECT | *God focuses on what can be done in the present instead of dwelling on what I should have done in the past.*

Day 165 Becoming Adventurous

READ | Isaiah 43:19
See, I am doing a new thing! Now it springs up; do you not perceive it?

Can I let God do something new in my life? Can I set aside my fears and step out? New things in life scared me because I didn't know enough about them to control them. I wasn't skilled enough at them to be sure that they would build up my faltering self-esteem.

Now that I'm addressing these issues, I am freer to try new things. I can learn to serve a volleyball. I can take art lessons. I can speak in front of others. I can make friends with someone who doesn't talk about food and diets. I can eat healthy foods (like Brussels sprouts) without disgust and tasty foods (like butter on my toast) without guilt.

When I experiment, I may stumble upon one more piece of God's will for me.

God, show me your paths and give me the courage to follow them—even if they look new to me.

REFLECT | *When I try something new, I can allay my fears and dabble in serenity.*

Day 166 Overreacting to Criticism

READ | Isaiah 51:7
Hear me, you who know what is right. . . . Do not fear the reproach of men or be terrified by their insults.

I react to other people's criticisms in extreme ways. Sometimes I assume they must be true because I'm so inadequate, so I whip myself until I'm bloodied.

At other times I defend myself over and over until I'm sure I've convinced them that their criticisms aren't true (or perhaps I've just convinced them that I'm defensive). Afterward, I continue to rehearse my defense-attorney speech, and they rehearse the reasons they never want to talk to me again.

I'm finally learning to listen to critics, thank them, and go on. Then I ask myself if the criticism is useful. I sit on it a few days, and sometimes God brings to my mind instances in which the criticism was true. At other times I figure out that it is not true and I forget it.

God, help me stop overreacting to criticism.

REFLECT | *I can decide if a criticism is valid and respond appropriately.*

Day 167 The Shame of the Past

READ | Isaiah 54:4
Do not be afraid; you will not suffer shame. Do not fear disgrace;
you will not be humiliated. You will forget the shame
of your youth.

I relive some of the events of my past because I feel
such shame about them. Some are foolish things I did when
I was younger, and I regret them because I know I deeply
hurt people. As I make amends and forgive myself, the
shame goes away.

Other shameful events were not my fault, but I felt
shamed anyway because people were hostile toward me.
In some instances I confront those who mistreated me and
created this shame. In other instances, I accept that they
are bound up in shame themselves. I start working at forgiving these people.

I need someone as powerful as God to release me from
my shame. As I surrender each shameful event to him, he
releases the humiliation from them. I don't feel the sting of
the shame so keenly.

I surrender the shame of my past to you, God.

REFLECT | *I work through my past with the purpose of*
releasing the shame.

Day 168 Side-by-Side Shepherding

READ | Isaiah 56:11
They are shepherds who lack understanding; they all turn to their
own way, each seeks his own gain.

130

As a recovering fixer, I have tried to shepherd people without understanding their problems. In retrospect I see that I was simply trying to get them to do things my way. My gain was the subtle grandiosity of managing others' lives, often mixed with healthy attitudes of wanting to help them.

I'm abandoning this savior complex and choosing instead to walk beside others as they experience struggles. I offer no answers, although I may offer my experience, strength, and hope. I pursue shepherding relationships and friendships that are mutually helpful, and I share my mistakes readily.

This way involves less work and is more enjoyable. I see why it works.

God, please place me as a shepherd in the relationships in which you want me, but keep me from fixing.

REFLECT | *Part of helping others is respecting them.*

Day 169 God's Work of Art

READ | Isaiah 64:8
Yet, O LORD, you are our Father. We are the clay, you are the potter; we are all the work of your hand.

I am a work of art and nothing less. My value comes from the fact that I am made by the earth's Creator, and he is my Father. It's true that I don't always do everything right, but God expects me to make mistakes and loves me anyway.

If I focus only on how the world views me, I will feel worthless and unacceptable. When I understand that I am

131

the work of God's hand, I see that my disappointments and setbacks are used by God to turn me into a one-of-a-kind container.

I believe that God has a use for me even though I may not be aware of it. As his plan unfolds, I commit myself to enjoying him more and abandoning my disordered eating.

Thank you for creating me with such care.

REFLECT | *I am God's work of art.*

Day 170 Hooked on Control

READ | Jeremiah 9:8
With his mouth each speaks cordially to his neighbor, but in his heart he sets a trap for him.

Controlling others takes many forms such as coercing, manipulating, shaming, flattering, and talking behind people's backs. I trap them into becoming the people I think they should be because I think I know what is best for them. If I'm successful, I may force them to detour from the person God wants them to be. I am not surprised that they become irritated.

Learning to eat sensibly, live well, and love God involves giving up control over my friends, my relatives, and especially those to whom I am an authority figure. I go the extra mile to avoid controlling my children or those I supervise. I present desired behaviors and consequences, and I administer consequences when necessary. But I can never crawl into their hearts and change them. Only God can do that.

I surrender my compulsive controlling to you, Lord.
You can be in charge.

REFLECT | *I can enjoy others more if I leave them with their freedom of choice intact.*

Day 171   A Recovering Know-It-All

READ | Jeremiah 9:23–24
Let not the wise man boast of his wisdom or the strong man boast of his strength or the rich man boast of his riches, but let him who boasts boast about this: that he understands and knows me . . . declares the LORD.

I got myself enmeshed in my eating problems by thinking that I knew it all about eating and weight control. Even though it's apparent to me that my wisdom and strength are small, I still get the idea that I have the answer. I think I can solve all my problems myself.

When I surrender, I admit that none of my grandiose ideas work. I admit that I'm not holding out for one more miracle diet or dazzling self-help book to relieve my problem. I admit that only God, a power greater than myself, can change me.

This surrender weaves itself throughout my life. Because I know I'm not an expert, I listen to others more. Because I'm no longer my own god, I find it easier to worship God.

I surrender my need to be wise and clever to you, God.

REFLECT | *Knowing it all kills; surrendering it all renews.*

Day 172 Growing in Confidence

R E A D | Jeremiah 17:7–8
But blessed is the man who trusts in the LORD, whose confidence is in him. He will be like a tree planted by the water that sends out its roots by the stream. It does not fear. . . . It has no worries in a year of drought and never fails to bear fruit.

My fears are many; I fear abandonment and intimacy; I fear failure and success. I have backed off from friendships in fear of rejection.

Because I'm choosing to trust in God, I can be confident. My roots are deeper now; I know that my confidence is rooted in how God values me. My years of drought are less panicky; I'm learning to cope with things I cannot control. My seasons of bearing fruit are lengthening; God is using me in ways that amaze me. I am growing in the confidence I've wished for all my life.

Help me give each fear to you, God.

R E F L E C T | *I am not a person of great confidence, but I have great confidence in God.*

Day 173 Hope for the Future

R E A D | Jeremiah 29:11
"For I know the plans I have for you," declares the LORD, "plans to prosper you and not to harm you, plans to give you hope and a future."

The ups and downs of my disordered eating patterns convinced me that there was little hope for my future. As

I turn myself over to God, the veil of lies I've been telling myself is lifting and I can see ahead.

Now I see that when everything is crumbling around me, I can cling to the fact that God has given me a future and a hope. He actually has plans for me—the one who has been enslaved to food. Nothing is hopeless with God, not even the worst circumstances.

Jeremiah spoke the words in today's verse to people who would be taken captive, but even they had a future and a hope. That means that there is always a reason to get up tomorrow, a reason to get dressed, a reason to plan my day. God will work, and my hope will be rewarded.

God, help me to believe in this hope for the future
that you have given me.

REFLECT | *God supplies hope when I have no hope.*

Day 174 Letting Go of Fatigue

READ | Jeremiah 31:13
*Then maidens will dance and be glad, young men and old as well.
I will turn their mourning into gladness.*

Sometimes I feel guilty when I celebrate my progress. Life has been such serious business that I'm more comfortable feeling tense and fatigued!

I've learned that I can respond to tension by listing the things I am thankful for. I am thankful that I admit I have a problem with food, that I am not alone in my struggle, and that I surrender my anger and fears to God.

This helps me relax. Although I'm not the person I want to be, I'm not the person I once was. I can pause to think about how exciting this is. The pages of my journal show how much I've changed. I am making a turnaround from mourning to gladness.

God, help me let go of the fatigue and tension of the past.

REFLECT | *Gratefulness soothes my fatigue.*

Day 175 Personal Boundary Lines

READ | Jeremiah 39:17–18
"But I will rescue you on that day," declares the LORD; "you will not be handed over to those you fear. I will save you; you will not fall by the sword but will escape with your life, because you trust in me," declares the LORD.

I feel as if I need to be rescued when I am around those who violate my boundaries. I don't like insisting that others respect my choices or feeling as if they are living their lives through me. Some people expect me to reveal feelings and thoughts inappropriate to our relationship, and I feel invaded.

I need God's help to stand up for myself and assert my independence. It's as if I need a giant wrestler to be my guardian angel. I call on God, take a deep breath, and assert myself politely. Others aren't always pleased when I do this, but I am learning to respect myself and keep the boundaries of my familiarity with others intact.

God, help me to treat others appropriately and to be unafraid to request the same of them.

REFLECT | *To respect my own boundaries is to respect myself.*

Day 176 Insomnia Blues

READ | Lamentations 2:19

Arise, cry out in the night, as the watches of the night begin; pour out your heart like water in the presence of the Lord.

I used to view sleeplessness as an intruder, and I would eat a snack or take a pill to make myself drowsy again. Now I listen to what's going on inside myself without panicking that I won't get enough sleep to be fresh the next day.

These moments often flourish into heart-to-heart conversations with God about what I need to do or what I can't do anything about. I bring these things to him, and under the cover of darkness, I am free to cry and say my piece.

I'm trying to make friends with my insomnia by using wakeful moments as a valuable time of peace and silence to pray about things I never have time to pray about during the day. Sometimes, in this grand state of peace, sleep sneaks up on me.

Help me not to resent sleeplessness but to use it.

REFLECT | *God will nurture me even through the night if I let him.*

Day 177 Every Morning Is New

READ | Lamentations 3:22–23

Because of the LORD's great love we are not consumed, for his compassions never fail. They are new every morning; great is your faithfulness.

137

Morning can be a friend. I wake up with the energy I couldn't find when I went to bed. I have an opportunity to start over. My slate is clean, and I can begin again. My problems of yesterday are just that—problems of yesterday.

This isn't just wishful, sunshine thinking. This is reality. A piece of my old self has died in the night and I have been restored. Now is my chance to commit my eating plan to God and see how much serenity I can live in today. This is one of many ways that God gives me grace.

Thank you, God, for times to start over.

REFLECT | *God's grace allows me to start over whenever I need to.*

Day 178 Self-Examination

READ | Lamentations 3:40
Let us examine our ways and test them, and let us return to the LORD.

Eating compulsively seemed necessary to me because I wasn't good at facing reality, especially my character defects. As I make a searching and fearless moral inventory of myself, I discover the root character defects that cause my problems: self-pity, resentment, laziness, and fear of rejection. These defects tainted my attitudes and diminished my opportunities for healthy relationships and meaningful work. I used them to survive just as I used my disordered eating. Yet they hurt me when I thought they were helping me.

In order to become whole, I surrender these character defects. I can clear my conscience today by confessing these defects and beginning to work through them.

God, show me the ways my character defects trip me up
and how they make it difficult to follow your will.

REFLECT | *The path to normal eating patterns is through a
cleared conscience.*

Day 179 Trials in the Mind

READ | Lamentations 3:58, 60
*O Lord, you took up my case; you redeemed my life. You have seen the
depth of their vengeance, all their plots against me.*

I am haunted by destructive, negative thoughts that
tell me I am doomed to be compulsive, I am ugly, or I am
not good at anything. If I stop listening to lies and call on
God to help me fight the battle, he says, "Your life can be
changed. You are beautiful the way I created you. You are a
significant person."

I need to hear these truths over and over. I need for
God to act as my persuasive lawyer and sway me, the judge,
into believing that I should not be condemned and locked
away. Even when I dig up my past and spread it across
my mind, God can banish it with the thought that he has
redeemed my past.

Rescue me from destructive thoughts.

REFLECT | *Compulsive behavior can be short-circuited by
focusing on the truth.*

Day 180 Parental Legacies?

R E A D | Ezekiel 18:14
But suppose this son has a son who sees all the sins his father commits, and though he sees them, he does not do such things. . . .

If my parents overeat, am I doomed to overeat, or will I betray them by not overeating? If my parents are obsessed with thinness, can I be otherwise?

I have many of the positive and negative qualities of my parents. Although the pull is strong to imitate their negative qualities, I can choose to look at life differently. God sees me as a separate person from my parents. I can choose the kind of person I want to be and ask him to help me become that person.

God, please help me set aside lifelong tendencies that block wholeness.

R E F L E C T | *With God's help, I choose for myself who I will become.*

Day 181 Dry Bones Can Live

R E A D | Ezekiel 37:2-3
I saw a great many bones on the floor of the valley, bones that were very dry. [God] asked me, "Son of man, can these bones live?"

Even with an eating problem, I appeared to be such a together person. I wanted to be that, and I pretended to be that. But inside I was a valley of dry bones. I was worn out from trying to fill the desperate neediness within me. None of the food I was stuffing myself with could ever nourish those bones. When I began to look to God and to others for help, this was my way of asking, "Can these bones live?"

The prophet Ezekiel obeyed God's instructions to preach to the bones even though that sounded ridiculous. In the same way, I am exposing my broken body and heart to words of hope. As I write a moral inventory and make amends, the bones come together and tendons and flesh appear. God is waking me from my grieving state as I begin to live again.

God, thank you for not giving up on me.

REFLECT | *With God's power, even the driest of lives can be revived.*

Day 182 Dark Memories

READ | Daniel 2:22
He reveals deep and hidden things; he knows what lies in darkness, and light dwells with him.

As I face my eating problems, I remember events from childhood and adolescence that disturb me and explain my neediness. I remember how these eating patterns first began, and I feel sad. I trust God to reveal these things as I need to know them, and to show me the value of remembering them.

Even though some events are dark and painful, I view them now through the light of what I can learn from them. When I share them with others, I do so to overcome the hold they may still have on me. I don't blame anyone, but I want to know what kinds of things cause me to turn to food for survival. I don't have to be scared by these memories because I trust that God is the one who reveals them to me and I can ask him to help me view them with his wisdom.

God, help me see the pain in my past that has driven me to eat. Please free me from it.

REFLECT | *God is more powerful than my past.*

Day 183 In the Fire

READ | Daniel 3:25
Look! I see four men walking around in the fire, unbound and unharmed, and the fourth looks like a son of the gods.

The fourth man walking through the fire with Shadrach, Meshach, and Abednego is the same man who walks through my fires with me—Jesus Christ. Just as they walked in a fiery furnace without being burned, I am learning to walk through the fires of life without being overwhelmed.

Sometimes I wish God would simply snatch me out of the fire, and at times miraculous coincidences remove me from fiery situations. But I know that my wish is part of my old tendency to escape unpleasant things. Seeking wholeness means walking through the fire and surviving. Perhaps that's an even greater miracle.

Thank you, God, for walking with me
through problems.

REFLECT | *I walk through problems, not around them.*

Day 184 Roadblocks

READ | Hosea 2:6
Therefore I will block her path with thornbushes; I will wall her in so that she cannot find her way.

God has a way of hedging me in so that the wrong choices aren't available to me in some of my neediest moments. This happens when there is nowhere to buy food or no way out of eating dinner with someone.

At first I feel frantic when I cannot find what I think I need. Then I feel as if God is winking at me and saying, "Hang on for just ten minutes more, and you'll be OK." So I hang on for ten more minutes, praying or calling a friend, and I'm OK.

As I look back on these hedged-in moments, I see God's grace at work. I was weak, but he was strong.

God, thank you for seeing ahead of me down the road and preparing roadblocks when I need them.

REFLECT | *Some of my roadblocks are gifts from God.*

Day 185 Choices in Rage

READ | Hosea 11:9
I will not carry out my fierce anger, nor will I turn and devastate Ephraim. For I am God, and not man—the Holy One among you. I will not come in wrath.

When I feel the rage well up inside me, it's as if I have no choice. It must be expressed, and usually toward the person who angers me. This verse shows me the inner struggle of God with his own rage. Ephraim (the nation of Israel) turned her back on God, and this made God angry. Yet God chose not to "come in wrath."

I can make a choice similar to his. As I feel the rage well up inside me, I can choose to punish the person who deserves it or I can set the rage aside. I can determine the wisest course of action and pursue that. With my human limitations, however, I may have to get away to vent my anger in a healthy way so I can make my choice with a clear mind.

Thank you, God, for showing me your inner struggle
with your own anger.

REFLECT | *I can choose to imitate my heavenly parent, God, whose anger is not destructive.*

Day 186 God's Compassion

READ | Joel 2:13
Return to the LORD your God, for he is gracious and compassionate, slow to anger and abounding in love, and he relents from sending calamity.

When I was clinging to my strange ways of eating, I was so blinded by my own judgmental attitudes that I saw God as mostly a judge. I stretched it to the point that I sometimes saw him as a brutal task-master whacking people on the backside with a stick for not doing as they should. I imitated my inaccurate image of God by judging others and myself harshly.

As I stop judging myself without mercy, I experience God's grace and his deep mercy toward me. I find the compassionate side of him that I've overlooked. When I'm sure he is upset with me, I find that he is slow to anger and is abounding in love. All these discoveries are waking me up to spiritual truths I missed before: God works in me. I don't have to be exhausted and miserable to please him.

Thank you, God, for waking me up to parts of you I overlooked.

REFLECT | *God's compassion is often underestimated.*

Day 187 Indifference

READ | Amos 6:1, 4, 5
Woe to you who are complacent. . . . You lie on beds. . . . You dine on choice lambs. . . . You strum away on your harps. . . .

I never intended to be complacent. At some level, I cared about others. I felt bad when others hurt. But I was hurting so much on the inside that I dismissed others who could meet my needs. If being with someone interfered with my being with food, that person lost. The drive to feel good was so strong that I sacrificed the feelings, the self-esteem, and at times the well-being of those I loved in order to get my needs met. I was complacent by default; I didn't have enough time or energy to care.

As I turn away from my obsession, I find moments to pay attention to people I formerly missed. I find a new energy and excitement for causes I previously felt were hopeless.

God, forgive my complacency and help me look beyond myself and my needs.

Day 188 God Listens

READ | Jonah 2:2
In my distress I called to the LORD, and he answered me. From the depths of the grave I called for help, and you listened to my cry.

Is God listening? Is anyone paying attention to the mess I've made? These are the questions I used to ask from the depths of my despair. I asked God to help me escape, but I didn't think he was listening.

Now I see that God was listening, but that it was my turn to make a move—to become desperate enough to give up my obsession with eating, looking thin, and feeling good. When I called out to God, he answered me in many forms— support groups, supporting friends, books written by fellow strugglers like me.

Throughout my journey, God listens. He hurts with me and honors my attempts to surrender it all to him.

Please, God, continue to hear my cries
and help me know that you are answering them
even when I don't feel sure.

REFLECT | *Calling out to God is part of my healing.*

Day 189 Surprised by God

READ | Jonah 2:8–9

Those who cling to worthless idols forfeit the grace that could be theirs. But I, with a song of thanksgiving, will sacrifice to you.

I began to pursue ways of changing my life because I wanted to let go of my uncontrollable eating behaviors. I am surprised that I am experiencing a spiritual awakening as well.

No matter how much I asked for God's help with my eating problems, nothing seemed to happen. I felt as if God had deserted me. I see now that I was clinging so tightly to my worthless idol (my driven eating patterns) that I missed the ways in which God reached out to me. He tried to persuade me to surrender myself to him.

So now when I begin to feel deserted by God, I don't let too much time pass before I go to him. I spill out these feelings as well as my desire to renew our relationship. As a result, I find myself awakening to God.

God, thank you for helping me wake up to you.

REFLECT | *The more I surrender my relationship to food, the more I discover about God.*

Day 190 Food-Based Friendships

READ | Micah 3:5

. . . if one feeds them, they proclaim "peace"; if he does not, they prepare to wage war against him.

Some of my relationships are so closely tied to my old eating patterns that they are disintegrating. As long as these people and I laughed about our disgusting behaviors, we felt close and there was peace. We felt bonded, too, as we practiced our character defects together—gossiping, blaming others, and feeling sorry for ourselves.

Now that my old eating patterns are dying, these old relationships are dying, too. The bonds are gone, and I don't know if the relationships will survive. I'm not willing to go back to my unhealthy behavior to save them.

I can hope and pray that the relationships find a sounder footing in other common interests, but I am prepared that they may not. This is not the prettiest part of becoming whole, but it sometimes happens.

God, I surrender my relationships to you.
Help me discern if any are based
on the wrong foundations.

REFLECT | *I can survive the loss of who or what was entangled in my eating problems.*

Day 191 God Priorities, My Priorities

READ | Micah 6:8
He has showed you, O man, what is good. And what does the Lord require of you? To act justly and to love mercy and to walk humbly with your God.

I want to be able to distinguish core issues from peripheral issues. I want to focus on what is important, such as the following.

- Justice: I can act justly by being honest about my failings and not blaming my problems on others. I can admit my faults and make amends to those I have harmed.
- Mercy: I can love mercy by giving myself and others a break. I can reach out to newcomers and stragglers.
- Walk with God: I can walk humbly with God by taking time to pray, meditate, and read Scripture. I can surrender each person or circumstance I want to control.

I put time and energy into these God-focused priorities and let other peripheral issues take care of themselves.

God, help me have the same priorities you have.

REFLECT | *I will major in the major issues and minor in the minor issues.*

Day 192 Not Down Yet

READ | Micah 7:8

Do not gloat over me, my enemy! Though I have fallen, I will rise. Though I sit in darkness, the LORD will be my light.

Falling into my old eating patterns sets me back only if I choose to let it. I can fight back and tell my eating mistakes not to gloat over me! I may be knocked down, but I'm not knocked out. I may be wandering in the dark, but I'm fumbling for the light switch.

Breaking my new patterns of eating doesn't mean I'm finished. It means I will start again and continue one day at a time. My slips teach me where my weaknesses are, but now I can recognize them sooner. This is a minor setback, not the end of the world.

God is more powerful than the drivenness inside me. His love tells me to get up, brush myself off, and surrender to him all tendencies to beat myself up.

Thank you, God, for your compassion and kindness when I fall.

REFLECT | *Healthy eating patterns may be interrupted, but I can start over the next minute.*

Day 193 Combat Duty of the Heart

READ | Nahum 2:1

An attacker advances against you, Nineveh. Guard the fortress, watch the road, brace yourselves, marshal all your strength!

It takes a while to become savvy about when and where attacks on my progress to wholeness occur. I have to watch the road ahead. Holidays are supposed to be fun, but they can be so filled with stress that I want to give up. Any kind of transition puts the fear of the unknown in me. When relationships sour for no apparent reason, I feel confused.

During these pitfall moments, I prepare myself by journaling more, keeping with me a list of telephone numbers of people I can talk to, and reading books that remind me of spiritual truths. More than ever, I invite God into each event of the day and ask him for the serenity I need to survive. I confess my negative attitudes and my heart hunger as soon as I detect it.

God, help me recognize my pitfall moments early so I
can arm myself.

REFLECT | *Recognizing a slippery place for what it is, is*
half the battle.

Day 194 Writing It Down

READ | Habakkuk 2:2
Then the LORD replied, "Write down the revelation and make it plain
on tablets. . . ."

Nothing is so plain as when it's written down. I find
out what's behind the traffic in my head when I write down
my feelings in a journal. I discover hidden facets of myself
when I look back on my life and write an inventory of my
eating behaviors and what character defects have been
behind them. Some of this embarrasses me, but I can be
proud of my honesty. I can silently write what I cannot say
out loud. In putting simple pen marks on the page, I find
the clarity I need.

God told Habakkuk to write down the revelation he
would give him so it would be plain to Habakkuk and
others. By rereading my inventories and my journals, I see
plainly how I am changing. I see God's grace at work in
me, and I become even more determined because of the
incredible struggles I have endured. I return to my world
refreshed and confident.

God, help me find healing as I take an inventory and
write in my journal.

REFLECT | *Writing helps me face my feelings and work*
through them.

Day 195 Deciding Against All Odds

READ | Habakkuk 3:17–18

Though the fig tree does not bud and there are no grapes on the vines, though the olive crop fails and the fields produce no food . . . yet I will rejoice in the LORD.

Habakkuk's agrarian culture depended on budless fig trees and grapeless vines for food to survive. Their barrenness meant that some would have little to eat, but Habakkuk made a decision to rejoice in God anyway.

In the same way, I make decisions in spite of the odds against me. At this moment I may want to overeat, but I decide not to give in to that drivenness . . . one moment at a time. I feel like complaining, but I decide to call a few people and see how they're doing. I don't feel like going to a weekly meeting, but I decide to go anyway just to help out.

I'm glad for these decisions even if I sometimes grit my teeth and pray, "Lord, help me fake it till I make it."

God, help me make a habit of making these tough
pivotal decisions correctly.

REFLECT | *Making healthy decisions is half the battle.*

Day 196 Going on the Heights

READ | Habakkuk 3:19

The Sovereign LORD is my strength; he makes my feet like the feet of a deer; he enables me to go on the heights.

In my former busyness, I tried to prove I was a can-do, worthwhile person. But all that proving of myself left me empty inside.

Now that I'm giving up on my own strength, abilities, and will power, I find myself on the heights and I'm not sure how I got there. The progression of events is the same:

- I consider doing something healthy.
- I turn it over to God and ask if it's his will.
- If it is, I agree to try it, but I surrender it to him.

The result is that I take risks out on the heights and find myself miles ahead of where I was. People congratulate me, and I'm dumbfounded. It has been a struggle, but God has moved me along.

> God, keep taking me to exciting places in life
> where I've never been.

REFLECT | *To follow God is to prance on the heights.*

Day 197 Totally Loved

READ | Zephaniah 3:17

The LORD your God is with you, he is mighty to save. He will take great delight in you, he will quiet you with his love, he will rejoice over you with singing.

It's good to know that someone in high places likes me. Someone of importance considers me important.

I can't get enough of hearing that God, the all-powerful one, delights in me. He sees something within me of great value, and he smiles with delight at what he sees.

When I need to be rocked back and forth, he quiets me with his love and sings. Today's verse says he rejoices over the frail, human me with singing! I have his undivided attention, and I am the object of his love.

This focused attention quiets my neediness and gives me hope. I can recover from my unhealthy eating. I can know what it means to be valued and loved by others, even by myself.

Thank you for cherishing me.

REFLECT | *To be loved by God is my highest compliment.*

Day 198 The Needy Personality

READ | Haggai 1:5–6

Give careful thought to your ways. You have planted much, but have harvested little. You eat, but never have enough. You drink, but never have your fill. You put on clothes, but are not warm. You earn wages, only to put them in a purse with holes in it.

I never have enough. Whether it's food or clothes or money, I'm always looking for something more: one more taco to eat, one more outfit to wear, one more adult toy to show off. These things will solve everything—or so I think.

I'm giving careful thought to my compulsive ways. I'm tired of planting so much and harvesting so little. I want to fill this vacuum in my heart with something that satisfies my neediness on a continuing basis.

As I surrender this neediness to God, I grow in the sense that he loves me, and I, in turn, am able to see my value, usefulness, and purpose in life. With this in mind,

I do without the taco, the outfit, or the adult toy—for today.

God, I surrender to you all my attempts
to fill my neediness.

REFLECT | *My needs plus the love of God equal enough.*

Day 199 Trying Harder Doesn't Work Anymore

READ | Zechariah 4:6
"Not by might nor by power, but by my Spirit," says the LORD *almighty.*

People have said, "Use a little more will power!" I tried following that advice for years, and it worked for a while. Then my will power began slipping, and I felt terrified. Now I feel as if I have no will power at all.

That's why the process of surrender rescues me. Since my unhealthy eating patterns outlived my will power, I see that I will not recover based on my own strength or the cleverness of some new eating plan.

As I let go of my need to be sufficient and show my strength of will, I see how powerful the Spirit of God is. I don't have to try, strain, or fuss anymore. I can surrender to the one who has the power to do for me what I cannot do for myself. I am where God wants me—surrendered.

God, I acknowledge that my struggle with my
compulsion will not be resolved through my power,
but by your Spirit.

REFLECT | *Trying harder will never be enough.*

Day 200 Who Am I Doing This For?

READ | Zechariah 7:5

When you fasted and mourned . . . was it really for me that you fasted?

For whom am I trying to resolve my eating behavior? Am I changing to please a parent, a spouse, or a would-be spouse? Am I going to all this trouble so people will like me more? Am I hoping to conquer my problems so I can be more successful in my career?

The nation of Judah did good things (fasting and mourning) and said these actions were for God; but they were for show. God wanted Judah to do the right things for the right reasons.

If I'm facing up to my strange ways of eating now in order to please someone else, it does not work. I cannot abandon this eating behavior, which has been my emotional support, unless I am desperate enough to want to change. I choose to change because I know it's the best thing for me.

God, don't let me kid myself about
whom I'm changing for.

REFLECT | *I can set aside others' wishes and opinions and follow what I believe to be God's leading.*

Day 201　Playfulness Returns

R E A D　|　Malachi 4:2

But for you who revere my name, the sun of righteousness will rise with healing in its wings. And you will go out and leap like calves released from the stall.

As I sense a decrease in the drivenness of my eating, I find new freedom. Much like a calf released from its stall, I feel like kicking up my heels.

I can relax more because life isn't so tense. I am free to make friends with whomever I like without worrying about whether a person is thinner, cuter, or richer than I.

I can trust my instincts because I'm doing what's best for me instead of what feeds my old destructive relationship with food.

I am learning what it means to find serenity.

My feelings of uselessness, self-pity, and selfishness are decreasing.

Finally, I don't fear life so much.

Thank you, God, for the many benefits of following you.

R E F L E C T　|　*I am learning not only to eat sensibly, but also to participate in life.*

Day 202　Powerful Tools for Change

R E A D　|　Matthew 4:3

The tempter came to him and said, "If you are the Son of God, tell these stones to become bread!"

The tempter says similar things to me, such as, "Because you've been so good, have an ice cream cone between meals (or something else to break your resolve)."

Jesus often fasted, and that can be an effective spiritual discipline for communing with God. Eating sensibly becomes something of a spiritual discipline for me when:

- I surrender to God each suggestion the tempter makes;
- I practice healthy eating to regain life, not to lose weight;
- I am accountable to a supportive mentor and friends; and
- I examine my fear, anger, and self-pity and how they affect my eating.

Then I can be content to let stones be simply stones.

God, help me see eating sensibly as a spiritual
discipline.

REFLECT | *Healthy eating is one of several tools to help me gain a renewed life in God.*

Day 203 God's Bread

READ | Matthew 4:4
Jesus answered, "It is written, 'Man does not live on bread alone, but on every word that comes from the mouth of God.' "

Jesus might have said to me, "Man does not live on bread [and candy bars] alone . . . " because he knows I've tried doing just that.

Now I'm finding nourishment in the words and wishes of God as well as in nutritious food. I need to read about how God worked with fallible, flawed people in the Bible and helped them achieve his purposes. I need to see how he interacted with all of these people so I can understand him as the compassionate, yet demanding God that he is. I need the comfort, reassurance, and encouragement I find in God's Word. I need to discover and review healthy principles for living life. I need to be reminded of my priorities so I can make wiser choices about my time and energy.

God, help me recognize my need to
understand your Word.

REFLECT | *God's Word provides the instruction and motivation I need.*

Day 204 Admitting Powerlessness

READ | Matthew 5:3
Blessed are the poor in spirit, for theirs is the kingdom of heaven.

As long as I thought I had spiritual insight, I was impoverished. I thought I could find my way to God by pleasing him and feeling guilty and working harder every day. None of that worked because I was attempting to be spiritual.

My past eating problems help me see that my own efforts to control my body and to be spiritual are futile. Instead of drawing me closer to God, these efforts drive me away from God.

I'm learning to admit the poverty of my spirit: I am powerless to make myself a spiritual giant; I am powerless to make myself a normal eater; I am powerless to become a content person. I relinquish all these things to God, and I know he will make them come to pass in his time and his way.

> God, I give you my weaknesses and inabilities—I can hardly wait to see what you'll do with them.

REFLECT | *Spiritual paupers have enough sense to keep their eyes on God.*

Day 205 God Heals Within and Without

READ | Matthew 5:4–5
Blessed are those who mourn, for they will be comforted. Blessed are the meek, for they will inherit the earth.

I have felt depressed much of my life. I have spent hours and days grieving over the damage done to my body. I've let others push me around; I've even let my eating patterns push me around.

Jesus worked with crowds of people who were diseased and paralyzed, suffering severe pain and seizures, and he healed them of their physical infirmities. Then he blessed them and told them they would be comforted in their grief. He told them they didn't have to be pushovers anymore, but that they could be meek, meaning they could have quiet strength.

Jesus does a similar thing with me. Not only does he heal my body (although in a different fashion), but also he heals the deep neediness of my soul. He comforts me and gives me quiet strength.

God, thank you for addressing all my needs
—physical, emotional, and spiritual.

REFLECT | *God cares about the infirmities of my body, emotions, and spirit, and he heals me.*

Day 206 Useful in God's Eyes

READ | Matthew 5:13–16
You are the salt of the earth. . . . You are the light of the world. . . . Let your light shine before men, that they may see your good deeds and praise your Father in heaven.

Many times I feel worthless. But Christ says that I am salt—a flavorful, restorative substance—and I am light—a source of life for many. He gives me this identity because I have chosen him and nothing changes it.

Jesus tells me that I am salt and light even though I have an eating problem, I feel incompetent and unloved, and I have hurt others. He works in me to do his will in spite of my defects of character.

My problem is that I don't believe what he says about me. The more I believe him, the more effective he can be through me as salt and light.

God, I give you permission to do salt and light tasks
through me.

REFLECT | *I get my identity from who Christ says I am, not from others.*

Day 207 Asking Forgiveness

R E A D | Matthew 5:23–24

Therefore, if you are offering your gift at the altar and there remember that your brother has something against you, leave your gift there in front of the altar. First go and be reconciled to your brother; then come and offer your gift.

I often need to indulge in my destructive eating pattern when I feel twinges of guilt for having treated others badly. My appetite goes crazy when I can't look people in the eye because I've manipulated them or lied about them. I can't practice eating sensibly when I know others have suffered for my laziness or impatience.

I can, however, clear away the guilt by asking forgiveness of the people I've wronged and making amends when necessary. As I zero in on my defects of character, God sharpens my conscience so I can see and admit how I have harmed others. He helps me differentiate between my healthy guilt over wrongs I've committed and needless shame over incidents that were not my fault. As I clear my conscience, I can normalize my feelings about food.

God, give me courage to ask forgiveness of
those I've wronged and grace to forgive
those who have wronged me.

R E F L E C T | *To ask forgiveness and to forgive others is to thank God for forgiving me.*

Day 208 The Less Said the Better

R E A D | Matthew 5:37
Simply let your "Yes" be "Yes," and your "No," "No"; anything beyond this comes from the evil one.

Too often I defend myself, make elaborate promises, and give lengthy explanations:

- I said that to you because I thought you thought. . . .
- I promise that I will never overeat again.
- I hope you didn't think that I meant. . . .

I see now that I've excused, promised, and explained to make people like me. But when I offer these explanations and promises in such an apologetic way, I am giving others the power that I should be giving to God. I invite others to judge me, and that's not good for anyone.

As I learn to answer to God for what I say, I find that he needs no explanations or promises. God knows my heart.

God, I acknowledge that you have the power to be my judge. Help me stop inviting everyone else to judge me.

R E F L E C T | *Lengthy explanations and promises are attempts to justify myself, but God has already justified me.*

Day 209 Pray for Whom?

R E A D | Matthew 5:44–45
But I tell you: Love your enemies and pray for those who persecute you, that you may be sons of your Father in heaven.

Who but God could have thought of prayer therapy? I struggle and squirm over trying to forgive those who have wronged me, and it wears me out.

But when I pray for those I resent—as God urges me to do—it helps me. I pray that God will change their hearts and enemy-like behaviors. I even ask God to benefit their lives. Sometimes I have to grit my teeth during this part: I ask God to give them the things I want for myself—enough money to live on, good friends, a job they will enjoy, and a family that gets along. When I pray for these things, my resentments begin to creep away. I understand more of their perspective, and I begin to hope the best for them.

God, help me pray for good things for those I resent.

REFLECT | *To pray for others is to care about them.*

Day 210 When Bad Things Happen

READ | Matthew 5:45
He causes his sun to rise on the evil and the good, and sends rain on the righteous and unrighteous.

I have let the bad things that happened to me poison my attitude toward God. Sometimes I've blamed God, thinking that he was picking on me. This distanced me from God, and I've used my old eating patterns to survive rejections, failures, and misfortunes.

Finding wholeness involves accepting reality in every area of life. One piece of that reality is that all humans here on earth experience sunshine and rain. That happier, sweeter life we all hope for will occur in the afterlife, not here.

As I accept this reality, I can make peace with God. Having bad things happen to me does not mean that God is picking on me or that I'm a bad person or that I have no faith. It means that my life is normal.

God, help me not to take personally the bad things that happen to me.

R E F L E C T | *Trials and struggles are not attacks from God, but simply dilemmas I need to face.*

Day 211 Secret Fun

R E A D | Matthew 6:3–4
Do not let your left hand know what your right hand is doing, so that your giving may be in secret. Then your Father, who sees what is done in secret, will reward you.

Secret good deeds can be fun. No one knows what I've done, and I can laugh in the corner with God. Only he and I know that he used me to do this good thing.

Secret good deeds can also help me forgive. If I'm frustrated with people, it helps me to help them. I may not be able to speak to them in civil tones, but if I button up their kid's jacket, help them put chairs away, or say something nice about them to someone else (taxing my creativity at the moment), I feel better toward them.

This is one form of the spiritual discipline of service. I serve others because Jesus did. Seeing how good this sometimes feels and how it helps me forgive, I see why Jesus recommended it.

Thank you, God, that doing a good deed in secret
can drain me of my need to be admired and
my need to resent others.

REFLECT | *To serve is to heal.*

√Day 212 Dejunking Prayer

READ | Matthew 6:7
*When you pray, do not keep on babbling like pagans, for they think
they will be heard because of their many words.*

When I start babbling a prayer, I stop myself in the
middle and say, "What does this mean? Is this what I want
to say?"

This is especially true with prayers I pray often, even
prayers such as the Lord's Prayer used at the end of my
group meeting. I need to pause before I pray and remember that I'm talking to God, the one who rescued me. I can
ask myself the following questions:

- What can I thank him for?
- What needs can I present?
- What faults can I confess?

Rather than being extra work, this little extra effort
results in an attentiveness to God that reduces my need to
babble at anyone!

Help me present my true self to you, God, in my prayer.

REFLECT | *In prayer I have the opportunity to be myself more
than at any other time in my life.*

Day 213 Enjoying This Moment

READ | Matthew 6:34

Therefore do not worry about tomorrow, for tomorrow will worry about itself. Each day has enough trouble of its own.

I worry about the future, about what I'll say to someone and what they'll say to me. I worry about the past, about what was said and what I should have said. My tendency to live in the future or the past is a subtle form of escape, because it keeps me from doing anything today.

The daily tug of my desires to eat in destructive ways pulls me back to the present moment and reminds me to surrender one hundred percent of my attention to God today. I can stay put and work through today's issues. By the time tomorrow comes, things may change and I'll be better equipped to face them.

What a gift to enjoy today—to be thankful for the love of God and others and to be thankful for what I have and what I'm learning. I can feel more alive and enjoy my days more than ever.

Thank you, God, for today's moments and for the grace to enjoy them fully.

REFLECT | *I can be content and fully present in today's activities.*

Day 214 Judging

READ | Matthew 7:1–2

Do not judge, or you too will be judged. For in the same way you judge others, you will be judged, and with the measure you use, it will be measured to you.

When I meet someone with abnormal attitudes toward food or I hear someone in a support group say something childish, I can back up and take off my imaginary judge's robe. I don't know the whole story. I don't know the inner drives and thoughts of that person.

My role is to give people a break; God's role is to judge. I may observe characteristics about people, but I may not condemn or label them. I may pray for them, but I may not assume that I have diagnosed their problems. I may share my experience, strength, and hope when appropriate, but I may not act as another person's conscience. I'm busy enough reawakening my own conscience!

God, please help me hold my tongue and halt my thoughts when I judge others.

REFLECT | *The only person I can judge is myself—and then gently.*

Day 215 Perfectionism Denied

READ | Matthew 11:29
Take my yoke upon you and learn from me, for I am gentle and humble in heart, and you will find rest for your souls.

In my perfectionism, I act as if today's verse says, "Take my yoke upon you and groan from me, for I am harsh, and you will find exhaustion for your soul."

Perfectionism is harsh and exacting. There is one way to do anything and it's the most difficult, rigid way. Because I can never live up to this perfectionism, my neediness mushrooms, and I feel I have to quelch it with my compulsion.

To become healthy and remain that way, I must shed my perfectionism. I do this by openly admitting that I have a large, gaping sore—my eating patterns. That means I'm no longer a candidate for perfection, and I don't have to try so hard. Having admitted that, I can get on with important things in life such as growing in love, joy, and peace—one day at a time.

Thank you, God, for being so gentle. Help me to be gentle with myself.

REFLECT | *I can allow my eating problem to remind me that I am loved and cherished by God just as I am.*

Day 216 Considering God's Timing

READ | Matthew 12:14–15
But the Pharisees went out and plotted how they might kill Jesus. Aware of this, Jesus withdrew from that place.

My eating patterns taught me to act according to my feelings and my hunger. Jesus set aside his feelings and made decisions based on God's timing. Early in his teaching career, he avoided confrontation so he could have a few years to train the disciples. Later he confronted the religious leaders, allowing himself to be killed. This was God's timing for him.

I am learning to act rather than react based on what I think God's timing is. When I am accused, I try to determine if it's time to confront or time to let go. I can trust that there is wisdom beyond emotional reactions and revenge. I may not always understand God's timing or respond to it, but it's important that I at least consider it, asking myself, "Do I have peace about doing this now or responding this way at this time?"

God, help me try to consider your timing.

R E F L E C T | *I honor my feelings, but I don't let them rule my actions.*

Day 217 Words

R E A D | Matthew 12:36–37
Men will have to give account on the day of judgment for every care-less word they have spoken. For by your words you will be acquitted, and by your words you will be condemned.

Words can hurt. I have to ask myself, Would I make this comment about this person if he or she were standing in front of me? How do people feel about my repeating what they said? Often I choose to make amends for gossip, thoughtless judgments, and words I don't mean.

Behind my words are a thought life I have to account for as well. I'm most comfortable around people I love, and too often my unkind thoughts pour forth and hurt them. This thought life is slowly becoming more positive, but in the meantime, I want to check more carefully the words I leave hanging in the air.

I want my words to help instead. I want to use my tone of voice to offer warmth, respect, and even mercy to others.

God, please teach me to choose to speak to myself in a merciful way.

R E F L E C T | *My words are a practical barometer of the progress I'm making.*

Day 218 The Value of Solitude

R E A D | Matthew 14:23

After [Jesus] had dismissed them, he went up on a mountainside by himself to pray.

Jesus frequently went off for extended times of solitude with God. I'm discovering that I also need solitude. I need extended times of prayer, meditation, worship, and Scripture reading to renew me in a way that nothing else does.

Isolation, on the other hand, drains me. I used to build walls around myself and my eating patterns, and I spent a lot of energy refusing invitations, getting out of commitments, hating the thought of doing any work, and fearing that I would lie in bed forever and never get up again.

I'm sometimes so afraid of isolating myself as I have in the past that I fear solitude, too. But I don't let fear of the past keep me from spending time with God.

God, help me not to fear solitude because of the way I
punished myself with isolation in the past.

R E F L E C T | *Time alone with God restores me.*

Day 219 What's in It for Me?

R E A D | Matthew 20:26

Whoever wants to become great among you must be your servant.

As surrendering my neediness dismantles my drivenness for food, it dismantles my quest for power, too. Although

I've had pure motives for serving others, I've also enjoyed serving in order to have power over people. In this way, service propped up my flagging self-esteem—but if the service didn't go well, I felt defeated. After all, it didn't impress anyone.

Serving others with only their needs in mind feels empty at first. There's nothing in it for me, and I can't be concerned about myself. It means not letting my bad moods make me ungracious, and not caring whether anyone appreciates what I do. I serve only because I think this is what God wants me to do.

As I get used to this hands-off, selfless attitude, service becomes more enjoyable, and this is one more paradox of surrender.

God, please teach me to enjoy selfless service.

REFLECT | *I can serve because God prompts me to rather than to impress people.*

Day 220 The Gift of Touch

READ | Mark 1:40–41

A man with leprosy came to him and begged him on his knees, "If you are willing, you can make me clean." Filled with compassion, Jesus reached out his hand and touched the man.

Jesus healed other people without touching them. Why did he bother to touch this man whose disease stigmatized him as a social outcast? Perhaps Jesus was also healing the man's skin hunger, his desire to be touched, as he healed him of leprosy. Perhaps no one else had touched the man in years.

I, too, have had skin hunger for a healthy touch. People in support groups have hugged me and even held me when I've most needed it.

I can offer the gift of touch in appropriate ways that don't violate others' physical space. Some people like full-bodied hugs. Others prefer simple pats on the knee or on the arm. I can't be sure what a person needs, but I can follow my intuition and offer a healing touch as it seems appropriate.

God, guide me in using a tender touch
with people who need it.

REFLECT | *Touch can be a powerful nonverbal message of love.*

Day 221 Worry over What Others Think

READ | Mark 2:16
[The teachers of the law] asked [Jesus'] disciples: "Why does he eat with tax collectors and 'sinners'?"

Given the choice between dining out with admired leaders or common sinners, I would choose admired leaders. Jesus didn't. He cared nothing about impressing people. He knew who he was and why he was on earth.

I'm learning who I am and why I'm on earth. I'm a fellow struggler with many other people who are healing. I'm not here to impress anyone with a svelte figure or a magnetic personality.

As my self-respect grows, I care less about what people think of whom I see and where I dine and how old my car is. I put my energy into important things like becoming the person God intended, seeking God's purposes in my life, and knowing and loving others.

> God, help me find relief for my flagging
> self-esteem so I can quit worrying
> about what others think of me.

REFLECT | *I can replace my concern with what others think about me, with concern for what God thinks (and eventually I think) about me.*

✓Day 222 Being Freed

READ | Mark 5:3–4
This man lived in the tombs, and no one could bind him any more, not even with a chain. For he had often been chained hand and foot, but he tore the chains apart and broke the irons on his feet.

This man's story is the story of my path toward wholeness. The chains I used to control my unhealthy eating and dieting became weaker as my disordered eating advanced. The drive to numb out by eating or get high by excessive dieting then became stronger. It resembled the demon-possessed man's life: "Night and day . . . he would cry out and cut himself with stones" (v. 5).

Dabbling with the idea of giving up my eating behaviors is scary. As the demon-possessed man cried: "What do you want with me, Jesus? . . . Swear to God that you won't torture me!" (v. 7). The one who freed this man frees me. I am not being healed instantly, but it is a miracle, nevertheless, that I am being freed from the craziness raging within me and have the opportunity to discover real life.

Thank you, God, for making sanity possible for me.

REFLECT | *I can break loose from the chains of my eating behaviors.*

Day 223 Messiah Without a Messiah Complex

READ | Mark 6:31

Then, because so many people were coming and going that they did not even have a chance to eat, [Jesus] said to them, "Come with me by yourselves to a quiet place and get some rest."

How can I go off with my friends when there are so many tasks that need to be done and people who need help? That's my messiah complex talking.

It's interesting that the Messiah himself, Jesus, could take a break when he needed it. He even urged his disciples to come away with him to a quiet place.

I'm learning that God doesn't always want me to be a martyr, to do the hardest possible thing, or to be the most miserable I can be. He understands my need for rest, relaxation, and diversion. He wants me to balance my life between my work and my play, between myself and my family, and between being with others and being alone with him.

God, show me what I need to do to balance my life.

REFLECT | *I don't have to be a martyr to be loved by God.*

Day 224 Loving Confrontation

R E A D | Mark 10:21

Jesus looked at him and loved him. "One thing you lack," he said.
"Go, sell everything you have and give to the poor, and you will have
treasure in heaven. Then come, follow me."

Certain people who talk to me impatiently about abandoning my unhealthy behavior look detached and disgusted with me. When Jesus told this rich man to give up what he was obsessed with—his money—Jesus looked at him and loved him.

God sees me with my arms wrapped around my harmful behaviors and loves me anyway. At times I decide, as the rich young ruler decided, to hang onto my obsession. I may walk away sad as he did, but I remember the love in Jesus' gaze. And when I'm sick of my obsessiveness and ready to change, I remember the love. I know I'm welcome to come back and change my mind. So I do.

And I pray that when it's my turn to offer a similar challenge to others, I can do it with the love Jesus did.

Thank you for the love you have for me, God,
even though I am obsessed at times
with my eating behaviors.

R E F L E C T | *God looks beyond my obsession and loves me.*

Day 225 Rageless Justice

R E A D | Mark 11:15

Jesus entered the temple area and began driving out those who were
buying and selling there. He overturned the tables of the money
changers and the benches of those selling doves.

Although Jesus did get angry and frustrated at other times (and anger is not necessarily wrong), the Scripture doesn't say that he was angry in this instance. It's possible that Jesus, with his genuine, caring ways and finely tuned sense of justice, could overturn these tables of extorted money without anger or rage.

As I learn to cope with my emotions, I see that sensing an injustice doesn't have to be an emotionally charged issue. I may feel deeply about the issue, but I can set aside that blaming attitude and present the issue in a fair and reasonable way.

I can stand up for justice without raging on and on. I can be passionate, but fair. Even though I feel determined, I can be sensitive to others.

When I need to confront others, God, help me do so in a fair, helpful way.

REFLECT | *I can stand up for justice justly.*

Day 226 Is Food My God?

READ | Mark 12:30
Love the Lord your God with all your heart and with all your soul and with all your mind and with all your strength.

I've separated the parts of my life so much that at times my faith amounted to little more than visiting God weekly at church. In the meantime, my eating problem filled every moment of the day and took the place of God in my life. I worshiped food and thinness by the way it preoccupied my thoughts and dominated my actions.

As I'm prying the tentacles of my troubles with food off my heart, I have a new hunger for God. I want to love him with all my heart, soul, mind, strength, and—body! I want to consider him throughout the day. I want to dethrone food and come to know God.

God, teach me what it means to worship you in a way
that surpasses how I worshiped food and thinness.

R E F L E C T | *Whatever I center my life around is what I worship.*

Day 227 Looking Outside Myself

R E A D | Mark 12:31
The second is this: "Love your neighbor as yourself."

The team approach to recovering from destructive eating patterns helps me see outside myself. Others also struggle, and I long to connect with them and know them.

Because I feel a team spirit with others in facing my struggles with food and self-esteem, I am more aware of others. I wonder if the person sitting in front of me on the bus, the teenager sitting next to me in the doctor's office, and the executive across the restaurant are struggling, too.

I understand that I can't rescue everyone, but I can give of myself to those God puts in my path. I can pray for them, listen to them, and affirm the progress I see in them. I can offer them the acceptance I'm learning to offer myself.

God, help me become aware of the people you put in my path.

R E F L E C T | *Other people's struggles are as real as mine.*

Day 228 Asking for Help

READ | Mark 14:33–34

He took Peter, James and John along with him, and he began to be deeply distressed and troubled. "My soul is overwhelmed with sorrow to the point of death," he said. "Stay here and keep watch."

I'm afraid I'll bother someone if I ask for help, and I'm afraid that I'm not important enough to matter to anyone. My self-esteem is so fragile that I'm not willing to ask for prayer and companionship as Jesus did when he was overwhelmed in the garden of Gethsemane. Who am I to need less than Christ himself needed?

But asking others for help is appropriate. It's a step of growth for me because it requires the courage to approach others and the humility to admit my neediness.

God, give me the courage and humility to reach out to others when I need help.

REFLECT | *Reaching out for help is a sign of wisdom, not weakness.*

Day 229 Time Alone with God

READ | Luke 4:42

At daybreak Jesus went out to a solitary place.

The amazing thing about Jesus' going out at daybreak into the dew-dampened outdoors is that the previous day had been an exhausting one (Luke 4:33–41). He had recruited followers, driven out demons, and healed a lot of people. Why didn't he sleep in?

It looks as if Jesus slipped off to be with God the way two parents make time to sit up and talk after their children go to bed. Jesus, too, carved this time out of his schedule for fellowship and reflection with God.

I need quiet moments with God, too. I need to reflect on the direction my life is taking. I need to unload the long list of issues that trouble me and people and causes I care about. These extended moments set a tone of being aware of God so that in my normal events of the day I find it more natural to maintain conscious contact with God.

God, help me understand how much I need to
spend time with you, to enjoy it when I do,
and to be eager to do it again.

R E F L E C T | *That anxious emptiness inside me is a signal to spend time with God.*

Day 230 Respond Instead of React

R E A D | Luke 6:29
If someone strikes you on one cheek, turn to him the other also.

When someone insults me or picks a fight with me, my natural responses are fight or flight. I strike back with an equally powerful retort or I make an excuse to leave and feel hurt.

There is another choice. I can forgive the person and stick around. I don't stay to get beaten up or verbally abused, but I don't retaliate either. I don't fight and I don't flee.

If my child yells at me, I don't need to yell back. I can give a hug. If neighbors get upset with me, I can continue to treat them with kindness and concern.

I don't respond this way to win back their friendship. I do this because it's right to imitate Christ. I find that in the process I am not eaten up with resentment and anger, and I don't eat because of what's eating me.

God, help me learn the gentle art of surprising the resentment out of myself.

REFLECT | *Fire doesn't fight fire; water fights fire.*

Day 231 Courtesy and Self-Respect

READ | Luke 6:31
Do to others as you would have them do to you.

Being polite seems like an unnecessary frill in life, but I'm learning that it's one small sign of respect and self-respect. It's easy to feel I don't have time to be courteous to a sales clerk, a telephone salesperson, or a driver in the next car. Children are often considered unworthy of respect, but my politeness to them shows that I value them, and that builds their self-esteem.

Being polite also means that I respect myself and that I'm willing to impart some of my self-respect to others. I can respect others' words, wishes, and feelings. This is one more subtle way to leave behind my self-obsession.

God, help me reflect your grace in the way
I deal with people.

REFLECT | *Courtesy reminds me that God loves each person as a valued human being.*

Day 232 Unspoken Messages

READ | Luke 6:45

The good man brings good things out of the good stored up in his heart, and the evil man brings evil things out of the evil stored up in his heart.

I used to say to myself, *At least I didn't say anything; I only thought it.* I used to believe that I was progressing if I didn't verbalize the negative thoughts I was thinking. And maybe I was at that time.

But my nonverbal messages can be even more powerful than my verbal ones. When I entertain negative thoughts about people, the negative thoughts produce a resentment that makes me quietly ignore or snub them. Then I have to police every thought and every word. This life of hypervigilance is not a healthy one.

I want to dismiss negative thoughts about others as soon as they appear so I can become whole from the inside out.

God, help me store good things
in my heart about others.

REFLECT | *Good words and thoughts decrease the negative traffic in my head.*

Day 233 Never Enough

READ | Luke 9:25
What good is it for a man to gain the whole world, and yet lose or forfeit his very self?

In my efforts to feel good about myself, I have not only eaten and dieted excessively, I have searched for the good life. I have tried to feel acceptable by expending my energies trying to live an upwardly mobile lifestyle, wearing the right clothes, and pursuing a fast track in my job. My neediness forces me to feel I am hopeless without these things.

As I surrender this great neediness, the lure of these things subsides somewhat. Where I live, the clothes I already own, and my present job are good enough. I don't have to prove anything to anyone. God's will is becoming more important, so I spend more time on growing spiritually than on acquiring positions and prestige I don't actually need.

I want to love you, God, the Blesser, much more than I love your blessings.

REFLECT | *I can pursue God's will and set aside my need for money, fame, and power.*

Day 234 Do the Next Task

READ | Luke 9:54–55
When the disciples James and John saw this, they asked, "Lord, do you want us to call fire down from heaven to destroy them?" But Jesus turned and rebuked them, and they went to another village.

Letting go of eating struggles can be so exciting that I get big and bold ideas of what comes next, as James and John did. I decide I'm going to abstain from a new food, but I sense God telling me to simply make my portion smaller that night for dinner. I decide I'm going to start going to another meeting, but I sense God telling me to help the one I already attend.

It's not so much an either-or issue or even that I must always do the smaller, humble thing. It's that I can discern what is the next step in my life based on my responsibilities and limitations, not on what sounds impressive. There may be other times to dream big—as long as it's God's dream for me.

God, show me the next thing I should do and help me do it.

REFLECT | *Big ideas are great as long as they are the right ones for me.*

Day 235 Busy, Busy

READ | Luke 10:41–42
"Martha, Martha," the Lord answered, "you are worried and upset about many things, but only one thing is needed."

I have hurry sickness when I feel pressured to do many things in a short time. When I ask myself who is putting this pressure on me, it's often me. I have given myself goals and deadlines that are unrealistic. I would not be as hard on anyone else as I am on myself.

I'm learning that it's not a crisis if I do something tomorrow instead of today or if I'm late for a meeting. It's true that these imperfections let people know that I'm only human, but that's the truth. I'm not perfect.

When I'm not in such a hurry, I recognize my higher priorities more easily, such as the one thing that Martha needed: to spend time listening to Jesus.

God, thank you for never being in a hurry with me.
Please help me do the same with my life.

REFLECT | *I can listen to my priorities even if they differ from what seems to be most urgent.*

Day 236 Facing the Drivenness

READ | Luke 11:24, 26

When an evil spirit comes out of a man, it goes through arid places seeking rest and does not find it. Then it says, "I will return to the house I left." Then it goes and takes seven other spirits more wicked than itself, and they go in and live there. And the final condition of that man is worse than the first.

As I become more whole, my drivenness flares up in new, unexpected temptations and I have to face them. As I quit using food to fill my neediness, I may struggle with spending too much money or fantasizing about the star of the last movie I saw. The drivenness has to go somewhere, and I find damaging ways to process it. I need to face my drivenness and not let it express itself in other ways.

I face that drivenness by using my spiritual tools such as journaling, praying, meditating, and talking things out with friends. By using these tools, I can do more than stop the eating behaviors; I can work through the neediness behind them.

God, help me recognize when I'm simply exchanging
temptations instead of effacing my drivenness.

REFLECT | *My goal is to work through my neediness to be-
come a whole person.*

Day 237 Expecting the Worst

READ | Luke 12:22, 25

*Therefore I tell you, do not worry about your life, what you will eat;
or about your body, what you will wear. Who of you by worrying can
add a single hour to his life?*

With each financial setback, I see myself out on the
streets by tomorrow night. I think that if I expect the worst,
I'll feel better when it doesn't happen. Instead, I get myself
and others upset.

I worry because I have a difficult time trusting God.
Most of the things I fear never happen, but I am packed
for twenty-seven emergencies and armed with contingency
plans.

As I practice one-day-at-a-time living, fear of economic
insecurity is leaving me. I don't make things worse by
awfulizing life. Because I don't worry so much, I am emotionally prepared to meet calamity as it comes. I can be
myself and slide through the turmoil more easily. Some
would call this serenity.

God, teach me to view life through the lens
of trusting you.

REFLECT | *Trust can replace worrying and obsessing.*

Day 238 Answers in Unexpected Places

READ | Luke 13:24

Make every effort to enter through the narrow door, because many, I tell you, will try to enter and will not be able to.

The narrow door is surrender; the wide door is control. In the past, I have joined more diet clubs and health spas than I care to remember.

Diets and other food and weight-centered methods only increase the drivenness for a compulsive person like me. Now I stand at the narrow door of surrender, admitting that I'm powerless over my eating patterns and that only God can restore me to sanity.

I see that God often moves in the opposite direction of my culture. In giving up, I win. In surrendering, I overcome. It's OK to be different and swim against the current of my culture when I sense that I'm in God's will for me.

God, help me to be willing to go against
my culture's love of power and admit
my powerlessness.

REFLECT | *I am taking what may be considered an unusual route to wholeness, but I believe it is God's will for me.*

Day 239 Love That Risks

READ | Luke 15:4

Suppose one of you has a hundred sheep and loses one of them. Does he not leave the ninety-nine in the open country and go after the lost sheep until he finds it?

Why would a shepherd abandon ninety-nine sheep in open country where there are wolves, in order to hunt down one sheep? This goes against logic.

What would make anyone willing to do this? Having what God has: an illogical love for each person, a dogged determination to do whatever it takes to help even one person find him and grow closer to him.

I am that one person, and God has illogically loved me in spite of my faults. He has refused to give up on me even when I've given up on myself and on him many times. This kind of love is a mystery to me, but I thank God for it.

Thank you, God, for picking me out and loving me, for coming to get me when I've been lost.

REFLECT | *I can accept God's determined, relentless love for me.*

Day 240 Inconvenience

READ | Luke 15:8

Or suppose a woman has ten silver coins and loses one. Does she not light a lamp, sweep the house and search carefully until she finds it?

What makes a woman look for a virtual needle in a haystack in the nighttime darkness of her Palestinian hut? Why not wait until morning?

Her methods, like God's methods, are not based on convenience, but on doing what's important. If I imitate God in this way, I must set aside my love for convenience when I pursue wholeness.

Going to weekly meetings is not convenient. Listening to struggling friends is not convenient. Eating sensibly is not always convenient. But I have set aside the softer, easier, more convenient way in order to pursue a way of life that will make me whole.

God, forgive me for my love of convenience,
and teach me to put first things first, as you do.

REFLECT | *I can imitate God by setting aside the love of convenience.*

Day 241 Talking to Myself

READ | Luke 15:17
When he came to his senses, he said, "How many of my father's hired men have food to spare, and here I am starving to death!"

Is it strange to plan what I'm going to say to myself? This worked for the prodigal son. After he squandered his wealth in wild living, he talked some sense into his own head.

I can use the same process to contradict my negative thinking with powerful truths about the way life really is. I can even use some familiar sayings:

- When I beat myself up: "Progress, not perfection."
- When I try too hard: "Easy does it."
- When I become impatient with myself: "One day at a time."
- When I make a big deal out of things: "Keep it simple."

This is how I can renew my mind day by day.

God, help me tell myself the truth—again and again.

REFLECT | *Self-talk can be self-renewing.*

Day 242 Facing Mistakes

READ | Luke 15:21
The son said to him, "Father, I have sinned against heaven and against you. I am no longer worthy to be called your son."

My mistakes don't cancel God's love for me. Like the prodigal son, I can always come home, take responsibility for my mistakes, ask for forgiveness, and crawl back into God's lap. I can count on God to restore me.

If I make a mistake, I can still come to God. Instead of saying, "I'm too ashamed, I can't pray," I can say, "I'm so ashamed, I must pray." Facing up to my mistake is the most healthy thing to do. I can trust God to help me.

I can confess my mistakes to my friends, too. Instead of feeling too ashamed to go back to a weekly meeting, I can admit that I need to attend and that I wouldn't dare miss it. I know that the others at the meeting are simply flawed persons just like me.

God, help me trust you and others
to forgive my mistakes.

REFLECT | *The times I choose to run away from God and from friends are the times I could be running toward them.*

Day 243 Crushed Faith

READ | Luke 22:31–32
Simon, Simon, Satan has asked to sift you as wheat. But I have prayed for you, Simon, that your faith may not fail. And when you have turned back, strengthen your brothers.

Simon Peter was sifted and crushed when he was tempted to deny Jesus. Jesus prayed for Peter, but this was an odd prayer. He could have prayed that Peter wouldn't be tempted or hurt, but instead he prayed that Peter's faith wouldn't fail.

Peter failed by denying Jesus, but his faith didn't fail. He didn't give up on God. He later reconciled with Jesus and went on to be a great disciple of Christ.

I have been sifted by my eating problems. I have felt crushed by them and weary with God. I have failed, but in a sense, my faith hasn't failed. As I've come to the end of myself, I've realized that no matter how bad things get, I need God to get through. My faith is strained, but it's surviving.

Thank you, God, for helping me sustain at least some faith throughout my struggles with eating.

REFLECT | *My faith in God may grow dim, but I don't need to let it die.*

Day 244 God, My Parent

READ | John 1:12
Yet to all who received him, to those who believed in his name, he gave the right to become children of God.

In addition to my human parents, God is my parent. He fills in the gaps in the human parenting I received. He is there for me no matter what. He does not shame me; he does not even try to control me. He even lets me wander off on occasion, and I have to find my way back.

Because God is my parent, I feel hopeful in spite of my past; God was there watching me, guiding me, and, at times, grieving over my behavior and things that happened to me. I feel hopeful for the present; what happens today is an important part of how God is restoring me. I feel hopeful for the future; God will help me become all that he has for me.

God, I want to celebrate being your child and knowing you.

REFLECT | *As God's child, I am never without hope.*

Day 245 Realistic Expectations

READ | John 2:23–24

Many . . . believed in his name. But Jesus would not entrust himself to them, for he knew all men.

I have depended on people too much. They might have promised with the greatest of intentions to help me but could not follow through. I felt disappointed, bitter, and needy enough to behave badly.

They could not follow through because they were only human. Some were bound up in their own insecurities and they didn't know how to give. Others were caught up in their responsibilities, and they shouldn't have made such promises. Still others had a change of heart and decided to withdraw their attention from me.

While I have often expected unrealistic things from people, Jesus knew that those who believe him today may turn on him tomorrow. I need similar wisdom. I don't want to ask people to give me more than they can deliver. That is only fair.

God, help me not to anticipate from others more than they are able to give.

REFLECT | *I cannot expect from people the total commitment I can find only in God.*

Day 246 Filled with Purpose

READ | John 4:34
"My food," said Jesus, "is to do the will of him who sent me and to finish his work."

When I do something that is meaningful to me, I can miss a meal and not notice it for a while. I don't even feel hungry. My hunger is assuaged by the purposefulness I feel when I'm doing something I like. I may be talking about important things with people or working on a project that engages me.

When I do things that imitate Christ—loving God and loving others—I feel fulfilled, and my drivenness nearly dies. It nourishes me, so to speak, because afterward I feel filled with energy and enthusiasm to do even the tedious tasks of life.

Thank you, God, for sharing your sense of purpose with me and for the way it feeds me.

REFLECT | *I find fulfillment in doing what God has created me to do.*

Day 247 Finding God

READ | John 5:39–40

You diligently study the Scriptures because you think that by them you possess eternal life. These are the Scriptures that testify about me, yet you refuse to come to me to have life.

It's possible to know Scripture and not know the God of Scripture. It's possible to memorize Scripture and not have surrendered to God. I can give God portions of my intellect as I read or study, but still hold back my whole self. Sometimes I may even use Scripture to beat myself up: "If I'm a new creation in Christ, why don't I act like it?"

Only as I surrender myself to God do I read Scripture with an understanding of who is talking to me. Then I am touched by his love for me, his plan for me, his example for me. Then I am bonded to the God of Scripture, and I find strength and assurance for myself.

God, help me pause before reading your Word and surrender myself to you first.

REFLECT | *A surrendered heart gives me clarity of vision.*

Day 248 Unleashing Food

READ | John 6:9,11

Here is a boy with five small barley loaves and two small fish, but how far will that go among so many? Jesus then took the loaves, gave thanks, and distributed to those who were seated as much as they wanted.

194

I tend to feel territorial about eating. It would be a radical thing to give up a candy bar I've saved for myself. It can sometimes even be difficult not to care about where I go out to eat with a friend. What if I have a fixation for a roast beef sandwich and she wants a salad instead? What if I'm being good and planning to have a salad, and he wants to go to a greasy-spoon place?

I'm learning to give up my possessive feelings toward food and food choices. Food is no longer my friend or enemy; it is simply a substance provided by God to nourish me.

As I watch this emotional attachment fade, I watch myself find nourishment in my contentment with life. It is not skimpy nourishment either. It is as much as I truly need.

Please, God, sever the bonds I have built with food.

REFLECT | *I can trust God enough to provide proper nourishment even if it's not what I had in mind.*

Day 249 Climbing Down Off the Pedestal

READ | John 6:15
Jesus, knowing that they intended to come and make him king by force, withdrew again to a mountain by himself.

Because I have tried so hard to please others, they think too highly of me. I've wanted to be honest, but it was difficult to share how broken I was and how I behaved in private with food. While I have liked being on a pedestal, Jesus stayed off it. He knew he was not an earthly king, so he didn't let the crowds treat him like one.

Climbing down from my pedestal means that I share my brokenness instead of letting people think I'm fine all the time. It means that I don't do things just to impress someone. Being transparent about my faults helps me remember that I am only human. And when someone else discovers that I'm not perfect, I don't feel so driven to prove otherwise.

God, don't let me forget who I am and what I've come through.

REFLECT | *Admitting weaknesses builds strength.*

Day 250 Judging by Appearances

READ | John 7:24
Stop judging by mere appearances, and make a right judgment.

People misunderstand my past drivenness to eat when they look only on the surface of things. They don't understand that it grew from a deep inner neediness. This shallow thinking leads to inaccurate conclusions:

- All overeaters are overweight. (Many do not become overweight, because they also diet continuously, or simply metabolize food differently.)
- The goal of eating sensibly is weight loss. (The goal is to stop unhealthy eating patterns.)
- The goal of seeking a new kind of wholeness is weight loss. (The goal is to live a surrendered life.)

God asks me to understand wholeness for all that it means. This helps me stop looking at outward appearances in the rest of my life, too.

God, help me look below the surface at motives instead
of outward appearances.

REFLECT | *I see others more clearly when I consider the
motives that lie beneath the surface.*

Day 251 Quick to Judge

READ | John 8:7
*If any one of you is without sin, let him be the first to throw a stone
at her.*

When I am eager to accuse someone, it's usually because
I have a problem similar to that person's problem. I get
exasperated with someone's negativity because I'm being
negative. I am horrified that someone is cheating on his
or her spouse because my thought life has not been true
to my significant other. My own faults not only cloud my
judgment, but they also heighten my sensitivity to others
who do the same things.

When I judge others for defects of character that I
possess, I go back to pretending that I am a flawless, perfect
person. I fall short of this every time and drive myself
down the road of discouragement. Wholeness involves
understanding that others are as bound up as I am and that
judging doesn't help them or me.

When I feel quick to judge, God, help me examine
myself and extend mercy to others.

REFLECT | *To show mercy toward others helps me better
understand God's mercy toward me.*

Day 252 Truth and Freedom

READ | John 8:31–32

If you hold to my teaching, you are really my disciples. Then you will know the truth, and the truth will set you free.

As long as I denied that I struggled with eating, I was not free to heal from it. Admitting the truth about myself frees me to do the subsequent footwork: find support, journal about my struggles, and practice healthful living.

Doing these things helps me discover more truth. Support teaches me the truth that others are flawed like me, and that frees me to quit beating myself up. Journaling about my struggles allows me to confess my defects of character, and that frees me to surrender them. The discipline of eating sensibly shows me how dependent I am on my eating behaviors, and that frees me to admit my powerlessness.

I don't need to fear knowing the truth anymore. Each time I learn more truth about myself, I can use it to free myself.

God, help me not to regard the truth as an enemy to fear but as a friend to be thankful for.

REFLECT | *More truth leads to more freedom.*

Day 253 Frustrations and Faith

READ | John 11:21

"Lord," Martha said to Jesus, "if you had been here, my brother would not have died."

I have complained to God as Martha did: "Why didn't you change that person's mind? Why didn't you put me in a different situation? Why didn't you help me?" My complaints arose from my narrow human perspective compared to God's larger global perspective.

I begin to make peace with God by asking him these questions in a direct way, as Martha did. I express my honest frustration and honest faith. I don't understand immediately, but at least I don't have to eat my way to numbness just to get through the day.

As if to end on a positive note, Martha added: "But I know that even now God will give you whatever you ask." I also try to add some expressions of faith to my fussing and fuming questions.

Thank you, God, that I can talk with you honestly.
Help me express my faith, too.

REFLECT | *God values my honest interaction with him.*

Day 254 I Need to Cry

READ | John 11:35
Jesus wept.

Weeping is one way I can imitate Jesus! Since I no longer numb out with food, I experience my feelings intensely and I need to release them. Crying is one way to do that.

Sometimes I withhold tears because I don't have the time to get away by myself, or I'm afraid of being an emotional misfit. But the tears can't be stopped. I break a glass I never liked and find myself sobbing. The tears aren't about the glass, they're about my relative with cancer, my friend who is moving away, and my co-worker who is angry with me.

I'm thankful for tears and how they often force their way through my steely facade. My body heaves and grieves along with my heart. Sometimes, as it happened with Jesus, it lets others know just how much I value them.

God, please use my tears to create a strong,
sturdy serenity within me.

REFLECT | *Crying is an underrated path to wholeness.*

Day 255 Turning It Over

READ | John 14:1
Do not let your hearts be troubled. Trust in God; trust also in me.

Many of my troublesome moments occur because so many things are beyond my control. I can't control my eating behaviors. Just when I think I'm improving, I order too much at a restaurant, so I gobble it down or throw it away. I lie about having eaten; either I say I didn't eat so I can eat again, or I say I did so I can refuse to eat without anyone catching on. My heart is troubled by my deception, and I can't seem to let go.

God tells me in the middle of my troubled moments to turn my hunger and turmoil over to him, so I do. If I take it back, I surrender it again. If I take it back again, I turn it over again by journaling or calling a friend. Gradually I turn it over more easily, a sign that I trust God more easily.

God, help me do whatever it takes
to put my trust in you.

Day 256 In His Name

READ | John 14:14

You may ask me for anything in my name, and I will do it.

I used to plead: "Please make me stop eating, please make me thin, please make me happy." What was missing? Why didn't it work?

I wasn't willing to do the footwork. I was hoping to use God as a magic wand, especially if I said the magic words, "In Jesus' name, Amen."

Jesus didn't mean for me to use his name as a magic wand. Asking in his name means that I'm seeking to follow God's will. And to follow his will, I need to put into practice the things I know are right: release resentments, support others, practice eating sensibly and living well. As I maintain conscious contact with God in prayer, I find that he fills my neediness and empowers me to turn my back on food for one more day.

God, help me follow your will by doing what I know
is right.

REFLECT | *I can trust that God is waiting and willing to meet my needs.*

Day 257 More Than Talk

READ | John 14:15–17

If you love me, you will obey what I command. And I will ask the Father, and he will give you another Counselor to be with you forever—the Spirit of truth.

My plateaus in this process occur when I talk a lot but don't use the tools. Sometimes I become stuck in anger and blame, going on and on about what others have done to me, but I don't work on forgiving and releasing.

Wholeness doesn't come when I'm all talk and no action. I must do a lot of both: talk, especially in weekly meetings; and action, especially prayer, meditation, reading, abiding by a sensible eating plan, and service to others.

After Jesus' tough talk about obedience, he offers me some help with my action: the Counselor, the Spirit of truth will come alongside me and peel away the layers of my denial. He will guide me so I can do more than just talk.

Thank you, God, for the Holy Spirit's help in putting muscle into my motives.

REFLECT | *Wholeness is to be both talked out and walked out.*

Day 258 No Fear of Abandonment

READ | John 14:18

I will not leave you as orphans; I will come to you.

The only person who will never leave me is God. He alone is capable of that kind of commitment to me. Even those who love me very much will often move away or be drawn away by other important commitments. As orphans are reluctantly abandoned through death, so will I be abandoned by other people.

God will be my only lifelong friend. He is never too busy for me and comes to me when I need him. I don't have to worry about appeasing him or trying not to irritate him. God is the one I can count on to stick with me until death—and beyond.

In the security that God meets my fears of abandonment, I can steady my panic and keep from grabbing food to calm me. There is someone to stick by me, and I have found him.

Thank you, God, for promising never to leave me and for being able to follow through on your promise.

REFLECT | *God is the only one who is capable of relieving my fears of abandonment.*

Day 259 God's Peace

READ | John 14:27
Peace I leave with you; my peace I give you. I do not give to you as the world gives.

The supposed peace my unhealthy eating gives me is tenuous at best. It is peace by escape, by avoiding trouble, by refusing to face things. When circumstances become overwhelming, the peace crumbles, and my eating cannot put the peace back together again.

God's peace is much more than the absence of trouble. It is a peace of conquest won by surrender. It is independent of outward circumstances. I can go to the doctor and be weighed on the scale and still have it. I can be around troublesome people and still have it. I don't have to go to the convenience store to get more of it. I can use my tools.

Thank you, God, for this multifaceted, powerful peace.

REFLECT | *True peace is steady and always available.*

Day 260 Connected to God

READ | John 15:5
I am the vine; you are the branches. If a man remains in me and I in him, he will bear much fruit; apart from me you can do nothing.

I have tried to have a beautiful body all by myself. I've spent portions of my life eating grapefruit and cottage cheese, busting the springs of gut-busting machines, and spending so much money on gyms and weight-loss programs that I could have bought beachfront property (which I would have hated anyway because I'm so anxious about how I look in swimming attire).

My drivenness to tinker with food is a spiritual problem that I can't resolve without the power of God. This drivenness has defined me by what I eat, and I need God to remind me that I am his child. I need his power to push away this eating behavior that is so tightly woven in the fabric of my days—and nights.

I surrender my clever techniques and choose to set up camp in God's shadow and to remain there, one day at a time, forever.

I admit, God, that I tried everything but surrendering
myself to you.

REFLECT | *Dwelling in God is the best place I can be.*

Day 261 An Important Friend

READ | John 15:15

*I no longer call you servants, because a servant does not know his
master's business. Instead, I have called you friends, for everything
that I learned from my Father I have made known to you.*

Being God's child makes me feel secure, but being a
friend of Christ is a little different. How can someone be
Christ's friend?

Understanding Christ's mission on earth positions me
as his friend. He came to set me free from my appetite, my
fears, and my anger. He and I gather for long talks in prayer,
and I begin to sense how much he wants me to overcome
my problems and how long he has been waiting for me to
do this.

I have quite a group of friends standing around me,
cheering for my growth—wise friends who counsel me, my
weekly meeting, and now, even Christ.

God, I feel honored and loved
to have Christ as my friend.

REFLECT | *I have a friendship with Christ as well as with
others.*

Day 262　Rebirth Cycles

READ | John 16:21
A woman giving birth to a child has pain because her time has come; but when her baby is born she forgets the anguish because of her joy that a child is born into the world.

Nonstop, smiling faith isn't real; life is full of painful moments. But as I work on finding wholeness after years of eating struggles, I watch my pain bring forth surrender, disciplined habits, and even a waning of my character defects. This is anguish.

I can hold on through this pain because I know what's coming. I know the joys of seeing a renewed person come forth. I'm different from my old self, and others can see it. I am regaining a normal body size. I have different eating habits. I have a more relaxed personality.

Because this is a lifelong process, these painful rebirths and joyful receptions occur over and over. If they stop, I stop growing.

God, I give you my grief because I anticipate the joy
that follows.

REFLECT | *Life is full of never-ending cycles of spiritual rebirths.*

Day 263　No Concern Too Small

READ | John 21:9, 12
When [the disciples] landed, they saw a fire of burning coals there with fish on it, and some bread. Jesus said to them, "Come and have breakfast."

Imagine Jesus, having just come back from the dead, surprising the disciples by cooking their breakfast on the beach. Even in his grand heavenly state, the physical hunger of the disciples concerned him.

Jesus wasn't so lofty and spiritual that he was unconcerned about the physical details of life. He supplied a good breakfast of fish and bread for the disciples. He's concerned with my down-to-earth needs and worries such as cars, computers, and rent payments. Even now he wants me to surrender the most practical or most inconsequential details of my life to him, even the ones I'm sure no one cares about besides me. He enjoys supplying what I need.

> Thank you, God, for being concerned
> about all my needs.

R E F L E C T | *God loves my total person and is concerned about my total needs.*

Day 264 Making the Pure Impure

R E A D | Acts 10:15
The voice spoke to him a second time, "Do not call anything impure that God has made clean."

The fuzzy thinking of my disordered eating led me to look at food in peculiar ways. For many years, a potato has been a bad food. Actually, a potato is a nutritious food, and it becomes a problem only when I load it with butter, sour cream, and bacon bits.

What other good things have I tainted because of my compulsive tendency? Are all weekly meetings bad because one of them was once filled with too much fixing and advice giving? Are all members of the opposite sex bad because one of them treated me badly? Are all books bad because I have escaped into trashy novels?

I need to shed this extreme thinking that throws the baby out with the bathwater—especially when the baby may be a person, activity, or thing that God has put in my life for my good.

God, help me respect the wholesome substances and activities you have provided on earth.

REFLECT | *I have access to clear thinking that recognizes unnecessary extremes.*

Day 265 Seeking God's Heart

READ | Acts 13:22

[God] testified concerning him: "I have found David son of Jesse a man after my own heart; he will do everything I want him to do."

What does it take to qualify as a person after God's own heart? It has nothing to do with being good enough. After all, David (the Old Testament king whom God praises in this verse) slept with a married woman and then killed her husband.

Being someone after God's own heart is a matter of loving God and following God's ways and will. What is that?

At least one part of God's will is to shed the bondage of my old relationship to food. He wants me to be freed from my preoccupation and guilt. Then I will be free to do the things he intends for me to do. I discover this by inviting him into my daily life over and over, surrendering my fear, anger, and self-pity as I go along.

He will let me know the rest.

God, I want what you want. Help me know what that is.

R E F L E C T | *To seek God is better than to try to be good enough.*

✓Day 266 Hooked on New Ideas

R E A D | Acts 17:21
All the Athenians and the foreigners who lived there spent their time doing nothing but talking about and listening to the latest ideas.

People wander into weekly meetings hoping to hear something new. They look disappointed when no one gives them advice or new insights. Nothing will be enough until someone waves a magic wand and takes away their problems.

Hearing new information is not enough. It doesn't solve my problems unless I do something with it. It's not the Scripture verses I don't understand that trouble me, it's the ones I do understand and am not willing to put into practice.

Becoming whole involves work. I talk things out and make myself accountable. I pray and maintain conscious contact with God. I write inventories and I journal. I put one foot in front of the other, surrendering each step to God.

Help me understand, God, that I will not get
better through obtaining new information but through
surrendering myself to you.

R E F L E C T | *I can push aside that desire for new insights and do what I need to do today.*

✓Day 267 Never Far Away

R E A D | Acts 17:27

God did this so that men would seek him and perhaps reach out for him and find him, though he is not far from each one of us.

When God seems far away, it's usually because I've put him there. I've blamed him and even resented him. But even when I distance myself from God, he makes himself known to me through people and books, through odd experiences and even the most ordinary ones.

God stands waiting nearby for me to reach out for him. He is never content to let me get too far away from him, even when I try to run away because I don't like what's happening and I take it out on him. He allows me freedom to wander, but he reminds me that I'm wandering away from one who loves and accepts me.

In time I see that I've separated myself from the one I need the most, from the only one who can help me. So I return, and he restores me in his love and confidence.

I come to you, God, even when I don't understand why you allow certain things in my life.

R E F L E C T | *God is the one to whom I can turn, not the one I should blame.*

✓Day 268 Giving Back Gives Back

R E A D | Acts 20:35

It is more blessed to give than to receive.

When I receive a telephone call from a needy friend, I feel bothered—for the first two minutes. As I listen and connect with what the person is saying, I hear my own struggles and fears being vocalized and I feel better myself.

Then I sit down and I may put my feet up. I relax and become interested in what's going on. I find that the words I say in response are the words I need to hear most. I gain insights I didn't understand before.

When I receive one of these calls, I'm being asked to give. And in giving, I receive.

God, help me to be receptive to the moments
I need to give.

REFLECT | *Giving becomes receiving when I have an empathetic heart.*

Day 269 A Clear Conscience Feels Good

✓READ | Acts 24:16
So I strive always to keep my conscience clear before God and man.

It's surprising how good it feels to do good things. A clear conscience begins to feel good, and as soon as I intentionally hurt people or feel jealous of them, I ask their forgiveness and get it off my conscience. This can be embarrassing, but it feels better than a guilty conscience. I like being honest before God.

This clear conscience makes it easier to speak up for myself at appropriate times. I'm not playing that old game, "Well, I didn't deserve the promotion anyway because of the way I treated so-and-so." When I deserve something, I can stand up for myself because I don't have negative baggage attached to the relationships. I feel free and clean.

Thank you, God, for showing me this new gift of
a clear conscience.

REFLECT | *A clear conscience is not only right, it's empowering.*

Day 270 Unexplainable Hope and Love

READ | Romans 5:5

And hope does not disappoint us, because God has poured out his love into our hearts by the Holy Spirit, whom he has given us.

I hobbled into this process of seeking wholeness after I had come to feel dead inside. My dieting, managing, and fixing had been thrashing me for years, and I felt beaten. It seemed impossible to generate any hope within myself.

Today's verse tells me that it's OK that I feel hopeless and loveless, because God is the one who generates an undisappointable hope and a flowing love. As I surrender myself, the Holy Spirit puts hope and love inside me without my realizing it.

There are days when I don't feel the hope and love, but I know they are there. I don't cry as hard and long as I used to. I reach out to others more easily. The gloom and doom is lifting. Yet I know that it's still the Holy Spirit putting this hope and love inside me. They sure aren't my own!

Thank you, God, for the hope and love you
pour into my heart.

REFLECT | *The hope and love God puts within me makes me*
want to continue to renew my mind and shed my compulsions.

✓Day 271 Deciding Against All Odds

READ | Romans 5:8

But God demonstrates his own love for us in this: While we were still
sinners, Christ died for us.

Most people wait until I show some promise before they're willing to go out on a limb for me. God didn't. He sent Christ to die for me even though the rest of the world viewed me as disordered, damaged goods.

Yet God scoops me up, confused, messed up and all, and declares me valuable—even before I surrender to him! He doesn't tap his foot impatiently and wait for me to be perfect before he loves me. He loves me now—while I'm still in my messy state.

When I do surrender, God's love empowers me to shed my old eating patterns. Much like the princess who kisses the enchanted frog, God loves me and equips me to turn into a prince of a person.

Thank you for loving me, God, when I haven't cared
about you.

REFLECT | *God doesn't wait for me to be good to go out of*
his way for me.

Day 272 Confusion

READ | Romans 7:15
I do not understand what I do. For what I want to do I do not do, but what I hate I do.

I am riddled with behaviors, habits, and feelings that confuse me. But that doesn't diminish my faith or progress. The Apostle Paul, who penned the words in today's verse, was a mature person who loved God and served him in dynamic ways. This confusion, then, is part of life. I must never become too proud or think I'm too perfect to admit my struggles.

Being transparent about my struggles is not a sign of weakness. It shows that I am no longer so plagued with self-doubt that I can't admit my problems. I keep sharing my struggles in order to get help. Even though I do things I hate, I am still in the midst of a lifelong process and I am still God's child.

Help me not to be overcome, God,
by my doubts and fears.

REFLECT | *A certain amount of doubt and fear is normal.*

Day 273 The Exact Nature of My Wrongs

READ | Romans 7:18
I know that nothing good lives in me, that is, in my sinful nature. For I have the desire to do what is good, but I cannot carry it out.

I tried "trying to be good." I tried to stop thinking about food. I tried to stop being moody and controlling. I kept all this bottled up within me and did my best. Nothing happened, except that I felt worse about myself.

Now I'm doing the opposite. I don't try anymore. I admit to myself, to God, and to others I trust that I am powerless over food, moodiness, and my desire to control. I no longer pretend to be OK.

I admit this not just once, but over and over, each time I obsess on food, feel moody, and think about controlling. I make it clear that I cannot carry out the good things I want to do. I can do nothing to improve myself. I can let go of my need to appear perfect, and I can ask God to take over from there.

> I am not you, God. I don't have the power to
> work out my own faults. I give them to you to work out.

R E F L E C T | *I admit the exact nature of my wrongs, and I surrender them to God.*

Day 274 Free from Condemnation

R E A D | Romans 8:1
Therefore, there is now no condemnation for those who are in Christ Jesus.

As far as God is concerned, I am free forever from condemnation because I am in Christ. Yet I keep viewing God as a shaming parent who is disgusted with me. I respond to this false image of God by condemning myself, heaping shame on myself, and considering myself useless.

I have wronged God in viewing him as a shaming ogre who is out to get me. Why do I do this? The spiritual enemy tries to convince me that God condemns me so I won't have the courage to think I can recover from my eating struggles.

I have a choice. I can resist these shaming thoughts about God. This is a day-by-day, hour-by-hour task. But it's worth it. I'm renewing my mind and finally finding that I am not condemned and that God is not a condemner.

Help me see you, God, for who you are and wipe away the false images I have put upon you.

REFLECT | *I am free forever from condemnation by God.*

Day 275 Self-Condemnation

READ | Romans 8:33
Who will bring any charge against those whom God has chosen? It is God who justifies.

Who will bring a charge against me? I will.

I have tried, convicted, and condemned myself. Sure, I know that Christ's death takes care of my sins in his eyes and offers hope and renewal, but I have a hard time believing it.

Now I focus on these truths day by day. When I remember the people I've hurt and the disgusting things I've done, I struggle to give myself a break. When I fall into old patterns of eating, I can choose to see clearly that I am loved in spite of the charges I bring against myself. Each day I beat myself up less and agree with God more that there are endless possibilities for me.

Help me, God, to show the same grace for myself
that you show me.

REFLECT | *I am free from even my own charges against
myself.*

Day 276 Nothing Disqualifies Me

READ | Romans 8:35
Who shall separate us from the love of Christ? Shall trouble or hardship or persecution or famine or nakedness or danger or sword?

In the past I have let my eating problems disqualify me as God's child. I figured that God couldn't and wouldn't love someone with a big problem.

The truth sinks in slowly. Nothing has been or ever will be powerful enough to separate God from his children—not divorce, not incest, not suicide attempts—nothing. He holds onto me as tightly as ever. Nothing I have done or that's been done to me marks me as an unlovable person. I can be fired from a prestigious job, I can be accused by my friends, I can be disowned by my family. All the things that shock people and make them gossip do not faze God. Nothing makes me unpromotable, undesirable, or unlovable to God.

God, help me to quit thinking that certain things
separate me from you.

REFLECT | *I can't do anything that would make God stop
loving me.*

Day 277 Telling God What to Do

READ | Romans 9:15
For [God] says to Moses, "I will have mercy on whom I have mercy, and I will have compassion on whom I have compassion."

I've had great ideas over the years of how God could solve my problems. I listed solutions for him: Change my grouchy neighbor's heart; cure my friend of cancer; make my spouse as devoted as the ones described in the how-to books on marriage. Some of these things happened and some of them didn't. I felt that God disappointed me too many times.

I see now that I have been using prayer as a weapon of control. I have tried to control God—as if that were possible!

With a surrendered attitude, I can bring my requests to God in a different way. I'm still fervent and consistent, but I don't have to tell God what to do. Instead, I watch, wait, and cooperate.

I admit, God, that I have had a power struggle with you. I will stop trying to control you.

REFLECT | *To accept God's sovereignty is one more necessary surrender.*

Day 278 A Living Sacrifice?

READ | Romans 12:1
Therefore, I urge you, brothers, in view of God's mercy, to offer your bodies as living sacrifices, holy and pleasing to God—this is your spiritual act of worship.

Because I'm a living sacrifice, I keep jumping off the altar. I keep coming up with new get-well-quick schemes: Maybe if I got this college degree or took this job or read this book or had a straight-A child, I'd be OK. Then I have to climb back on the altar and turn my problems with food, my self-worth, and my entire will over to God again.

I'm grateful for God's patience. I'm grateful that he calls this body I've abused with eating and dieting "holy and pleasing." He calls my turning it over to him my spiritual act of worship. That sounds pretty holy for an ordinary person like me. But that's why I turn it over. God is a power much greater than me, and he can restore me to the person he wants me to be.

> God, I turn my body, my will, my mind, and my emotions over to your care.

REFLECT | *I can trust God to do for me what I have not been able to do for myself.*

✓Day 279 Mind Renewal

READ | Romans 12:2
Do not conform any longer to the pattern of this world, but be transformed by the renewing of your mind.

The people I know and the magazines I read give me the message that overweight people are ugly and should do anything they can to become thin. The more I try to stop eating and dieting, the more I will hate myself.

I am in need of a major overhaul, a renewal of the mind. Simply trying new thoughts is not enough. I am learning to face my unpleasant feelings and my incorrect thinking. I can accept God's mercy and stop judging him. I can view people more realistically and interact with them more fairly.

My problem actually has little to do with food, and everything to do with the way I've chosen to manage the pain in my life. Renewing my emotions, mind, and spirit prepares me to accept reality and make better choices in life.

God, please renew my mind, my emotions, and my spirit, and teach me a pattern different from that of this world.

REFLECT | *An eating problem is as much about how I see myself as it is about how I eat.*

Day 280 Creating Chaos

READ | Romans 12:18
If it is possible, as far as it depends on you, live at peace with everyone.

Some people make a habit of creating chaos wherever they go. I am that way. I have been an excitement junkie—a little stab in the back here, a pile of complaints there. I was comfortable only if life was in an uproar. I want to change, yet I don't want to settle for peace at any price either.

Finally, I see the combinations I need. When confrontation is necessary, I can be affirming and gentle. When I have a strong opinion, I don't always have to express it. When things go wrong, I separate what is my responsibility and what is not, and I do my part and wait. I develop the best possible relationships with the people I know, but I accept that these relationships won't be perfect.

In this kind of peace, I find possibilities for genuinely positive excitement!

God, teach me to treasure peace without worshiping it.

REFLECT | *Peace is usually possible if I clean up my side of the street and let the other person clean up his.*

Day 281 Letting Go of Revenge

READ | Romans 12:19
Do not take revenge, my friends, but leave room for God's wrath, for it is written: "It is mine to avenge; I will repay," says the Lord.

As much as I'd like to think that no one in the world would wish me intentional harm, I've seen otherwise. Some people with control or power over me have taken advantage of me, lied about me, or tried to manipulate me.

I can work on releasing my desire for revenge as I trust that God is the author of justice and will dispense it as he sees fit. I can trust him to be just and to deliver the consequences in a fair and balanced way.

In the meantime, I can be relieved of the shame of grudges. I can forgive and go on. I don't need to knead my anger, and I can fight the temptation to wish someone the worst. I can let go of it, trusting that God will dispense justice.

Help me to trust you, God, to take care of those who have intentionally wronged me.

REFLECT | *Revenge is no longer as sweet as surrender to God.*

Day 282 Initiative

R E A D | Romans 12:21
Do not be overcome by evil, but overcome evil with good.

If I postpone overcoming evil, it overcomes me. In fact, just about everything I put off seems to overcome me. I think about a task and say I'll do it, but I don't. By the time I finally do it, I've already experienced the agony of it several times.

I am learning the value of initiative. A blossoming unhealthy behavior is much easier to deal with in its infancy. It's better to be on top of it than to let it flatten me.

I procrastinate because I'm afraid I'll fail or be rejected. So I gather courage (in case I succeed) and humility (in case I fail) and figure out what the next small step will be. By taking the next small step, minute by minute and day by day, I become what others call a self-starter.

Help me not to put off the things I need to do today.

R E F L E C T | *I don't have to do everything today—just the next thing.*

Day 283 Bureaucratic Blame Game

R E A D | Romans 13:1
Everyone must submit himself to the governing authorities, for there is no authority except that which God has established.

While I'm learning not to blame individuals for my problems, it's easy to blame impersonal bureaucracies. Government officials make mistakes, but I don't need to make them scapegoats. I still have personal responsibilities. My traffic violations are usually my problem, not the fault of law-enforcement officers. Even if corporations and government agencies are careless with natural resources, I can conserve the natural resources within my sphere of influence. I can take appropriate civic responsibilities such as voting, praying for officials, and paying the taxes I rightfully owe.

As I clear my conscience and dry up the guilt that my eating problems have fed on, I can take responsibility for my actions and my resources in every area of life.

> God, help me take responsibility for my own civic responsibilities and avoid blaming officials.

REFLECT | *I can improve my community by starting with myself.*

Day 284 Accountable to God First

READ | Romans 14:12
So then, each of us will give an account of himself to God.

I have committed my new way of eating and my defects of character to God. He understands my idiosyncrasies and why I need to practice the new habits I've chosen. And I don't expect anyone else, except perhaps my mentor or spiritual director, to understand my eating plan.

As long as I'm rigorously honest with myself, God, and my weekly meeting, I don't need to worry about what others think of me. But I do need to lay it before God on a daily basis so that he (possibly through my wisest friends) can help me see what I need to work on.

Reveal to me the ways I need to change, God, but help
me guard against the frivolous comments of others.

REFLECT | *My goal is to hear God's leading above the voices
of others.*

Day 285 Taking Someone Else's Inventory

READ | Romans 14:13
*Therefore let us stop passing judgment on one another. Instead,
make up your mind not to put any stumbling block or obstacle in
your brother's way.*

When I see others make mistakes or complain about
nitpicky things, what do I do? Do I question them and confront them? Perhaps I do in rare cases, but for the most part
I say to myself, "There, but for the grace of God, go I."

It's true. I have no right to take anyone else's inventory.
I have a problem with food and I'm surrendering it to God
the best I can. I have no time to take another's inventory
because I am busy enough using my tools and taking my
own inventory.

Besides, when I refrain from judging others, I don't
taint my role as their helper. When they are desperate or in
need, they know that I am available to help and that I won't
bring up negative events from their past.

Take away my need, God, to tear others apart.

REFLECT | *I am not the judge of my brother and sister, but
their fellow struggler.*

Day 286 Going the Distance

READ | 1 Corinthians 1:8
He will keep you strong to the end, so that you will be blameless on the day of our Lord Jesus Christ.

I have excelled in stops and starts. Sometimes my resolutions to eat properly lasted for a week or a month. At other times they lasted for a day or an hour.

As I commit my life to God one day at a time (one minute at a time on the really rough days), new possibilities open up. I see that with his strength and help I may eat sensibly and live well for a while, even through holidays and tough times. And when I do break my commitment, it's not the end. Because of God's empowerment in my life, I can call a friend or go to my weekly meeting and begin again.

This is new to me—to think that the paralyzing cycle of addiction could loosen its grip on me!

Thank you, God, for showing me the possibilities of beginning to iron out things that have plagued me my whole life.

REFLECT | *God's strength lasts for more than just a moment and beyond the next meal.*

Day 287 My Body—a Temple?

READ | 1 Corinthians 3:16
Don't you know that you yourselves are God's temple and that God's Spirit lives in you?

Contrary to what I have often thought, God considers my body a special item in his kingdom. He calls it—of all things—a temple.

Temples aren't to be worshiped, so I am careful not to worship my body by trying to make it as thin as possible or adorning it with things I can't afford.

But temples are to be maintained because they are places of worship. So I maintain my temple by eating nutritiously, getting enough rest and exercise, getting medical attention as needed. I keep the temple tidy by facing up to and cleaning out feelings of anger and self-pity, as well as self-destructive thoughts. I keep the flame on the altar of the temple well-lit by maintaining conscious contact with God all day long.

Thank you, God, for considering my body your temple.

REFLECT | *God values our physical as well as our spiritual being.*

Day 288　Advice They Can Do Without

READ ｜ 1 Corinthians 3:19

For the wisdom of this world is foolishness in God's sight. As it is written, "He catches the wise in their craftiness."

I can be a compulsive rescuer. I think to myself, *If these people would just do what I tell them, they'd be better off.*

My amateur therapist attitude turns my thoughts away from my own defects to those of others. Other people's thankful responses to my advice inflate my grandiose impression of myself.

I can't afford to give advice anymore. It deludes others because they relinquish to me their responsibility to get better. It deludes me because I begin to think their behavior and thoughts are within my sphere of control when they aren't.

In reality, I can change no one except myself.

God, help me to be more careful about rescuing others with advice.

REFLECT ｜ *I want to help others because God leads me to do so, not to feed my ego.*

Day 289　Slippery Places

READ ｜ 1 Corinthians 6:12

"Everything is permissible for me"—but not everything is beneficial. "Everything is permissible for me"—but I will not be mastered by anything.

The anything-is-OK-for-me, I-can-do-anything attitude gets me into trouble. I say that it's OK for me to eat five potato chips, but I munch through half a bag and a cup of dip. I agree to participate in a religious fast because someone who is very spiritual but very unknowledgeable about problem eating advises me to. I end up either over-eating or under-eating because I feel so deprived.

If I'm honest with myself, I know the foods and behaviors that persuade me to slip. So I name them and I make myself accountable for them. If I over-eat at parties, I either skip the next party or I take a friend who has similar problems with me the next time. These tools put the brakes on my slips and my I-can-do-anything attitude.

Help me, God, to recognize and become
accountable for the slippery places in my life.

REFLECT | *I need to make a habit of admitting my powerlessness, not testing my strength.*

Day 290 A Body That Honors God

READ | 1 Corinthians 6:19–20
You are not your own; you were bought at a price. Therefore honor God with your body.

I know that unbalanced eating and being overweight harm my body, so I have a difficult time believing that my body can honor God. Although I can't change what I've done in the past, I can do things differently today. Today, I can:

- surrender my food issues to God;
- surrender my needy feelings and thoughts to God and process them;
- surrender my defects of character to God;
- make amends to others as needed; and
- maintain conscious contact with God throughout the day.

I will not beat myself up for past mistakes or live in shame. God has forgiven me. I will honor God with my less-than-perfect body by changing my behavior today.

God, I surrender my abused body to you, knowing that you can restore even the most broken vessels.

REFLECT | *I can't change the past, but I can choose what I will do with my body today.*

Day 291 Common Struggles

READ | 1 Corinthians 10:13
No temptation has seized you except what is common to man.

From outward appearances, no one struggles as I struggle. No one has the same bulges or eating habits I have. No one feels as lonely as I feel.

When I start thinking this way, I need to be around other struggling people. I need to call a friend or go to a weekly meeting and hear others express the feelings of inadequacy that have haunted me. I need to hear them admit behaviors just like mine. I need to hear that their hurt runs as deep as my hurt, that they often feel they are alone on this planet with no one standing by them.

When I reach out, I laugh and cry and feel the loneliness in my body melt away. The isolation is gone.

God, help me reach out to someone like me today.

REFLECT | *In isolation I beat myself up; with support I pull myself up.*

√ Day 292 Keep On Keeping On

READ | 1 Corinthians 10:12
So, if you think you are standing firm, be careful that you don't fall!

It is possible to be vaccinated with self-control—to catch just enough that I never develop the real thing. After a few months of healthy eating, I considered relaxing the guidelines for my eating plan. Because I'd made progress with my major character defects, I thought I was qualified to pontificate.

I can and should celebrate my progress, but I must not forget where I've come from. My old eating behaviors took many years to develop, and they continue to lurk in the corner, monitoring my success. As soon as I think I've arrived, they are eager to creep forward and say, "If you're so great, how come you're still tempted by your old ways?"

So I stand firm. I look for more subtle character defects and temptations. I use my tools as much as ever. I keep journaling, calling friends, meditating, serving, and practicing eating sensibly.

God, help me not to let my pride stand in the way
of my growth.

REFLECT | *I use my progress to spur me on in the adventure of doing God's will.*

Day 293 Temptations of the Future

READ | 1 Corinthians 10:13
God is faithful; he will not let you be tempted beyond what you can bear.

The only way I can survive today is to give up panicking about the future. I give up my annual spring panic about looking decent in swimming attire. I give up my pre-holiday panic that I'll overdose on sugary goodies or stab one or more cantankerous family members.

I can also avoid panicking about whether God will fail me. Perhaps he's given himself too tough an assignment. Can he actually keep me away from overpowering temptations? For someone as compulsive as I, everything is a temptation.

I can absorb the truth of today's Scripture only if I don't look too far into the future. I can believe that for today God is able to help me stay on course.

Thank you, God, for being faithful today. Help me not to panic about the future.

REFLECT | *Most things I worry about never happen.*

Day 294 A Way of Escape

R E A D | 1 Corinthians 10:13
But when you are tempted, he will also provide a way out so that you can stand up under it.

When God closes a door, he opens a window somewhere. As I learn to trust God, I see that he cares about my healing and wholeness so much that he helps me continue it even when it looks impossible.

Sometimes I don't even look for the open window, the way out he provides. I bury my head so I can't see what's going on. Sometimes I do this intentionally because part of me fights the healing process. At other times I immediately look for the way of escape and take it.

I can't blame my slips on God. The truth is that I'm learning to be willing to take the way out he provides and to even enjoy it.

> God, help me become willing to use the
> escapes you provide.

R E F L E C T | *If I look for a way of escape, I'll find it.*

Day 295 The Nonperfectionistic Abstinence

R E A D | 1 Corinthians 10:31
So whether you eat or drink or whatever you do, do it all for the glory of God.

Eating for the glory of God? What is that? Is it facing food or the lack of it without any sense of neediness—a perfectly healthy attitude?

That's a tall order for someone like me. I'm used to appeasing my appetite, even my fixations. If I've gotta have ice cream, I've gotta have it. If I think that foods A, B, and C make me gain weight, don't even talk about them.

Eating for the glory of God is scary because it sounds so fuzzy. Will a bell go off if I goof? No, and that's the benefit. I can choose an eating plan that I think glorifies God. I may not keep that eating plan perfectly, but now I know that perfectionism doesn't glorify God. Justice and mercy glorify God, and I will reach toward my new goals with that in mind.

Help me choose an eating plan that glorifies you and use it with an attitude that glorifies you.

REFLECT | *A way of life that glorifies God is born out of surrender, not perfection.*

Day 296 Comfort from God

READ | 2 Corinthians 1:3–4
Praise be to . . . the God of all comfort, who comforts us in all our troubles, so that we can comfort those in any trouble with the comfort we ourselves have received from God.

I used to feel such bitterness toward God that I didn't allow him to comfort me. I was like a child who runs away, hides in her room, and buries her head under a pillow. Then I felt even more bitter toward God because he didn't comfort me.

All that is over. I can now turn to God and pray and cry in the shower and feel the tears flow with the water down into the drain. I can write in my journal and let the poisonous anger and hurt flow through my hand, into the pen, and onto the pages of my notebook. I can see the painful words lie dormant on the page and know that I have released them.

When I see that others need comfort, I try to listen to them as God patiently listens to me. I allow them to express their emotions, and I remind them that they are loved by God and by me.

Help me, God, to turn to you with my hurts.

REFLECT | *It is easy, but silly, to resist the greatest comforter of all.*

Day 297 Healthy Friendship Phobia

READ | 2 Corinthians 2:4
For I wrote you out of great distress and anguish of heart and with many tears, not to grieve you but to let you know the depth of my love for you.

When I back off from making friends, I think:

- If you knew the real me, you wouldn't like me. You would see my angry outbursts or crying fits and dislike me.
- If I were close to you, you could hurt me. You may ignore me, move away, or become angry with me. Then I'd hurt and use food to take care of that hurt.
- Being a friend involves work. I'd have to listen and consider your needs over my own. I don't have that much to give.

Before I can develop healthy friendships, I have to believe that someone else will value me. I have to have the emotional resources necessary to rally if that person had to leave me. I have to have crawled outside myself enough to be interested in someone else.

God, help me feel good enough about myself
to establish healthy friendships.

REFLECT | *My friendships will grow as my self-esteem improves.*

Day 298 Invisible Issues

READ | 2 Corinthians 4:18
So we fix our eyes not on what is seen, but on what is unseen. For what is seen is temporary, but what is unseen is eternal.

I have focused on something I can see and measure to sustain me—too much food, too little food. I have measured myself against others—Am I the right weight? Is she thinner? Is he more overweight? Am I more attractive? I have weighed and measured my way through too many diets. These actions don't work in the long run.

Now I focus more on the unseen. I see that my eating problems have spiritual dimensions and that I can examine the way I view God and how I think he sees me. I must figure out just whom I really depend on and why. As I work through these issues and surrender myself to God, I'm better equipped to eat sensibly and work through my problems.

God, help me see that my eating problems are riddled
with spiritual issues.

REFLECT | *Fixing my thoughts on what is unseen helps me maintain a proper perspective.*

Day 299 Newfound Freedom

READ | 2 Corinthians 5:17
Therefore, if anyone is in Christ, he is a new creation; the old has gone, the new has come!

Even though I have felt completely bound up in my eating struggles, I know that Christ has freed me to become a new creation. The essential battle has been fought, and I have been claimed as God's child.

The possibilities for me are endless. I have the freedom to choose to follow God's will in my life rather than the cycle of unhealthy behavior and despair. I am not absolutely bound up.

My responsibility is to walk in this freedom and grow. As I do so, spiritual reality becomes physical reality.

Thank you, God, for making me
a new creation in you. Help me walk
in that freedom.

REFLECT | *I am freed as a new creation, and with God's help, I can grow in that freedom.*

Day 300 God's Co-worker

READ | 2 Corinthians 6:1
As God's fellow workers we urge you not to receive God's grace in vain.

I am a co-worker of God because he and I work together now. I am surrendering my appetite, my drivenness, and my body image to God, and together we are working out my struggles. Together we are concerned about my growth in body, soul, and spirit.

As God's co-worker, I become concerned, as God is, about others' struggles and growth. I ask him how he wants me as his partner to help others grow. I make myself available as needed.

I see God's mission here on earth: to bring us together with him so we may know him and love him. I don't want this understanding to be in vain. I want to help others reconcile to him as opportunities arise.

> I enjoy cooperating with you. Help me
> follow your directions—
> and forgive me when I don't.

REFLECT | *God commissions flawed humans such as me to partner with him in his work.*

Day 301 When Sorrow Is Good

READ | 2 Corinthians 7:10
Godly sorrow brings repentance that leads to salvation and leaves no regret, but worldly sorrow brings death.

Worldly sorrow brings death because it is filled with shame, despair, and regret. There's no relief from this sorrow, so I sometimes fall into practicing my eating problem. That leads to more shame, despair, and regret. Depression chases me from corner to corner.

But when sorrow is godly, God's grace is mixed in it. I know that God pardons me and gives me what I need to start over. This grace allows me to examine my defects of character without beating myself up.

Godly sorrow turns me around. I reject my self-obsession and consider serving others. My inner restlessness tells me to seek God's presence and talk with him longer than usual. My deepest and finest decisions are made in moments of godly sorrow.

Thank you, God, for my godly sorrow and for speaking to me through it.

REFLECT | *Godly sorrow brings turning points in my life.*

Day 302 Stop, Look, and Listen Inventories

READ | 2 Corinthians 10:5
Take captive every thought to make it obedient to Christ.

I'm installing a symbolic trapdoor at the top of my skull. As a thought comes whizzing into my mind, I open the door, take the thought out, and examine it to see if it is healthy, reasonable, and godly. If so, I put it back in and let it do its work.

If not, I face it. I don't gag this captive thought and deny its existence. I treat it with respect and I listen to the feelings behind it. I may have to talk about it with someone else, but I don't let go of it until I face it head-on.

This type of intervention helps. I try to pray for my enemies before they become enemies and hand over resentments before they bloom into grudges. These stop-look-and-listen inventories save me anxiety later.

Teach me to face and process my negative thoughts.

REFLECT | *Intercepting a negative thought works better than curing it.*

Day 303 Comparisons and Competition

R E A D | 2 Corinthians 10:12

We do not dare to classify or compare ourselves with some who commend themselves. When they measure themselves by themselves and compare themselves with themselves, they are not wise.

"Her thighs are bigger than mine." "He eats three times as much as I eat." "My face is more attractive than hers." "He gets more laughs when he shares in our meeting than I do." Comparing makes for craziness.

If I'm honest, each of my comparisons is a self-esteem check. Am I OK today based on how I stack up against someone else? Or do I feel good about myself only if the other person looks worse?

I'm learning that I can be loved as I am, and I don't have to compete anymore. I measure myself against my own goals. I see my progress, I see my defects, and I set my face toward that maturity. I avoid becoming sidetracked by comparisons.

I look to you, God, for the measure of who I can be,
not to others.

R E F L E C T | *I'm needy when I compare. It's time to check my feelings and take a quick inventory.*

Day 304 Being Exploited Is Not Saintly

READ | 2 Corinthians 11:20

In fact, you even put up with anyone who enslaves you or exploits you or takes advantage of you or pushes himself forward or slaps you in the face.

Some have mistakenly said that the Christian thing to do is to be pushed around, exploited, and taken advantage of. The apostle Paul said this isn't true.

I'm glad Paul said that because being victimized makes me feel needy, and that inflames my old eating misbehaviors. I have to numb out so I don't hear the healthy drives inside me that say:

- You don't have to be loyal to people who don't merit loyalty.
- You don't have to try to please people at your own expense.
- You don't have to be abused physically or emotionally.

I have decided to stop placing myself in situations in which I am pushed and exploited. I take care of myself so I don't feel so demeaned that I have to eat.

God, help me change my course when I see an
unhealthy situation develop.

REFLECT | *To respect myself and ask that others respect me is a Christian attitude.*

Day 305 When Weakness Is Strength

READ | 2 Corinthians 12:7–10

There was given me a thorn in my flesh, a messenger of Satan, to torment me. Three times I pleaded with the Lord to take it away from me. But he said to me, "My grace is sufficient for you, for my power is made perfect in weakness." . . . For when I am weak, then I am strong.

"Haven't you taken care of that eating problem yet?" others ask me. I even ask myself this question.

For me, eating is a "thorn in the flesh." It is my lifetime reminder that God's grace is enough. It reminds me that when I am weak, God makes me strong.

My eating problems are my insurance policy that I will never again think I can do it all myself, that I will not fall into the trap of self-sufficiency, and that I will not forget whose person I truly am and whose grace saves me.

The thorn still hurts, but I can live with it.

God, thank you (I think) for this "thorn in the flesh."
Help me put it to good use.

REFLECT | *I live with a constant reminder to lean on God at all times.*

Day 306 A Servant, Not a Star

READ | Galatians 1:10

If I were still trying to please men, I would not be a servant of Christ.

When I served in the past, did I do it to earn points with God? to be admired by others? to feel better about myself? to feel worthwhile? Or was it a combination of these motives?

Now I know I live to please God first, not to impress others. When I want to be a star, I ask myself: Why am I doing this? Does it matter who knows I'm doing this? If it fails, will my self-worth be affected?

When I serve only because I'm a servant of Christ, I'm free to serve without building resentment. I don't burn out so quickly because I'm doing it for God and in his strength, not to feel better about myself. I use the gifts he's given me to fulfill purposes he's given. It's all in his hands.

> Help me, God, to serve others
> without self-consciousness.

REFLECT | *As I become less self-obsessed, my freedom to serve increases.*

˄Day 307 Rigidity

READ | Galatians 3:28
There is neither Jew nor Greek, slave nor free, male nor female, for you are all one in Christ Jesus.

Today's verse challenged its first-century readers to change their way of thinking and view people beyond the rigid categories of their culture. In the same way, recovering from an eating problem challenges my rigid categories, my harsh viewpoints, and my prejudicial ruts.

I don't identify people so much by how they are different from me but by what we have in common. I identify with the drivenness of the alcoholic. I see that Christians who approach their faith differently than I do may have something to teach me. I see that people throughout the world with very different customs and cultures want what I want: freedom to make a living and to be with those they love.

The result is that I'm less suspicious of others and more open to God's will.

God, save me from my former rigidity and help me to be absolute about only those things that are absolute.

REFLECT | *A rut is a grave with the ends kicked out.*

Day 308 Choking on Legalism

READ | Galatians 5:1
It is for freedom that Christ has set us free. Stand firm, then, and do not let yourselves be burdened again by a yoke of slavery.

Because I am good at making myself feel guilty, I am prone to legalism. When I hear others say they are giving up chocolate, I feel I should do the same thing. When I hear that others have written their inventory in a certain way, I feel I should do it that way to be right.

God doesn't send down a carton of size-five jumpsuits and say, "Anyone who can fit into these is OK." God is not a robot, and he doesn't ask me to be one, either. I am free to expand my relationship with him by asking him to show me the weight, healthy eating plan and wise friends that I need. Sure, I may hear him incorrectly, but he accepts that I'm human and prone to mistakes. He gives me the freedom to make these mistakes and correct them.

God, show me the weight, eating plan, and friends that
are most healthy for me.

REFLECT | *I am no longer in bondage to diets and weight
charts.*

Day 309 Restoring Others

READ | Galatians 6:1

*Brothers, if someone is caught in a sin, you who are spiritual should
restore him gently. But watch yourself, or you also may be tempted.*

Confrontation doesn't work unless I set aside my grandiose know-it-all attitudes. I can no longer play armchair
psychologist and diagnose every possible eating-troubled
person in town.

My goal and hope is to see people restored to wholeness.
I don't come with answers, I come with questions. I don't
come with solutions, I come with experience, strength, and
hope. I don't come with plans, I come with possibilities. I
lay these before my friend and let the friend take responsibility for her own behavior. I am simply one beggar telling
another beggar where to find bread.

I also know that as I say this to my friend, I'm bound to
face the same problem the next day.

God, give me courage to confront as needed, but help
me do so with gentleness and the same mercy toward
others that you show me.

REFLECT | *Not decimation, but restoration.*

Day 310 Burdens Are for Sharing

R E A D | Galatians 6:2
Carry each other's burdens, and in this way you will fulfill the law of Christ.

With my old attitude I would say, "That person sure is messed up!" With my new attitude I say, "That person sure is bound up."

It's a new thought to carry others' burdens instead of attacking them for their burdens. Instead of playing against them on an opposing team, I am trying to play on their team to see how I can help.

But how much can I help? God does the unbinding. I can listen, even at odd hours. I can invite them to come along with me at times. I can share my experiences so they know they are not alone. I can pray for them in their struggles. I can watch their burden be cut in half just by sharing it—and the joy doubled as they share that, too.

Teach me, God, to see others' burdens as something I
can help them carry, instead of reasons to attack them.

R E F L E C T | *My role is not to increase burdens, but to help carry them.*

Day 311 Magical Thinking

R E A D | Galatians 6:7
Do not be deceived: God cannot be mocked. A man reaps what he sows.

I have deceived myself in the past by believing in magical weight-control cures. I thought one more exercise gadget, quick liquid diet, or mind-control tape would do the trick. I have also deceived myself into thinking that eating junk food won't harm me. I've thought one more candy bar or bag of chips wouldn't make a difference.

I must ignore the magical thinking of my culture. Being thin doesn't solve problems, and pounds don't melt away! Part of becoming whole is accepting reality. Quick and easy solutions don't work because I have a physical, psychological, and spiritual problem. The only way to maintain proper weight is through a balanced diet and proper exercise. My body suffers when I eat a lot of junk food, no matter how little or unsalted it may be. That's reality.

God, help me face the realities of metabolizing food and maintaining proper weight.

REFLECT | *God does not bend physiological principles just because advertisers show pencil-thin people munching out.*

Day 312 Burnout Blues

READ | Galatians 6:9
Let us not be weary in doing good, for at the proper time we will reap a harvest if we do not give up.

I cringe to think of how I've strained and forced myself into rigid diets and exercise plans. I've spent a lot of time subtly pushing other people to do things. I've even told God what to do and when and where things should happen. All that straining and coercing doesn't work. When I give myself, others, and even God deadlines and nobody meets them, I become upset and burn out.

My effectiveness does not depend on how fast others do what I think they should do. What I think would be best may not even be best at all. When I lean on God's timing and trust him to do things in his perfect time, I don't become so weary. It's another surrender—my timing and my methods, for God's timing and God's methods.

God, help me stand by patiently as you do things in your time.

REFLECT | *Weariness is a sign that I'm taking on God's role, and I need to give it up.*

✓Day 313 Accepting My Personality

READ | Ephesians 2:10
For we are God's workmanship, created in Christ Jesus to do good works, which God prepared in advance for us to do.

My personality is different from the one I imagine the ideal person to have. Even though I make progress, I see that I have innate personality traits that seem to handicap me: I'm too high-strung. I'm not smart enough. I'm too shy. I'm too dull. I'm not a leader. I feel miles behind others.

Yet I recognize this attitude as more of the perfectionistic, magical thinking from the past. I am God's workmanship—even my personality. Like a tailor who creates a new garment, God created me with great care. Yes, I'm a little different from the rest, but that's OK. God urges me to continue to work on my defects of character, but not to be afraid to fulfill my purposes using the personality he has given me.

God, help me to see the advantages of my personality
and to continue to work on my defects of character.

REFLECT | *I accept the personality God gave me and I let
him work within it.*

Day 314 Self-Confidence

READ | Ephesians 3:12
*In [Christ] and through faith in him we may approach God with
freedom and confidence.*

At times my still-warped view of God makes me see
myself groveling, terrified, and shamed standing before
him. Approaching God with freedom and confidence is a
new idea. I'm free to express myself, and I'm confident that
he loves me.

This image of me as a free, confident person standing
before God gives me self-respect. I see that God respects
me, and I'm more able to quit shaming myself. I see that
the person in the mirror is not a fat cow but a child of God.
I see that I was not created to be talked down to; I can speak
up for myself. I see that I don't have to push and punish
myself; I can relax and enjoy times of leisure, too.

Since God respects me, who am I to do less?

Thank you, God, for respecting me and encouraging
me to feel free and confident.

REFLECT | *My confidence comes from God's view of me.*

Day 315 Gentleness and Patience

READ | Ephesians 4:2
Be completely humble and gentle; be patient, bearing with one another in love.

As I learn to be gentle with myself—to give myself time to rest and room to make mistakes—I can be more gentle with others, too. The more mercy I give myself, the more mercy I feel toward my children, toward my fellow strugglers and those I help. I can expect that people will make mistakes instead of being appalled by them.

When I become demanding, I can shift gears and slow down. When I question someone's motives, I can give them the benefit of the doubt. Like a gentle parent, I can confront others when necessary, but I don't do it because I feel impatient with them.

I can set aside my own drives and feelings for a minute to consider the other person. What a miracle!

God, help me grow in gentleness with others.

REFLECT | *Gentleness helps me get along with others and myself.*

Day 316 A Daily Choice

READ | Ephesians 4:22–24
You were taught, with regard to your former way of life, to put off your old self, which is being corrupted by its deceitful desires; to be made new in the attitude of your minds; and to put on the new self, created to be like God in true righteousness and holiness.

I can't simply fix my old self, so God offers me a new self. Having a new self doesn't mean I erase the hurts of my past, but I can be free of their hold on me and work through them.

Each day, each hour, each moment, I choose whether to resort to my old self or put on the new one. As the pain of my past presents itself in my mind, I can choose to acknowledge that former pain, forgive and make amends, and release it. Or I can choose to act on that pain with my past food behaviors.

Each little choice enhances or diminishes my overall choice to find wholeness.

When I feel discouraged, God, remind me that you give me choices to reject my craziness.

REFLECT | *Today's choices bring new opportunities, and I see that life is not hopeless.*

Day 317 Lying

READ | Ephesians 4:25
Therefore each of you must put off falsehood and speak truthfully to his neighbor, for we are all members of one body.

250

Lying seems like such an ugly thing—how can I admit to this? On the other hand, lying and deceit are a large part of almost every eating struggle. I've made it look as if I didn't eat when I did or that I did eat when I didn't. I've exaggerated when reporting my weight gains and losses. I've lied about how much I ate and I've claimed to have eaten only broccoli when I also downed half a bag of corn chips. I've lied to cover up my mistakes, and I've exaggerated my problems to get sympathy.

I can tell the truth now because I'm not so afraid of the flawed person that I am. Others who struggle with eating appreciate my honesty and even laugh at my distorted actions. Because of their love, I can present myself truthfully to others as well.

God, lift my shame, and enable me to tell the truth.

REFLECT | *I don't have to lie, because I am accepted as I am.*

Day 318 Anger Can Work for Me

READ | Ephesians 4:26–27
In your anger do not sin: Do not let the sun go down while you are still angry, and do not give the devil a foothold.

My anger itself is not bad; it's what I do with my anger that matters. If it gains a foothold in me, it can become destructive. If I nurse it, it will haunt me, make me hold grudges, and fester into hurtful comments. If I try to bury my anger, it will sour within me and turn into depression.

Anger can work for me or against me. I can face it by journaling my angry words, praying angry prayers, talking through my anger with my spiritual director or at a meeting, or even pouring my excess anger into playing music or sports. I don't have to let my anger control me.

This process also helps me see how I can use my anger for good. My righteous indignation can get me to stand up and get moving to do things I need to do but have not had the courage to do.

Help me face my anger, God, before it becomes destructive, and help me use it to motivate myself to do things I've been putting off.

REFLECT | *I can choose to make anger a positive force in my life.*

Day 319 Believing in God's Plans for Me

READ | Philippians 1:6
Being confident of this, that he who began a good work in you will carry it on to completion until the day of Christ Jesus.

When something good happens, I doubt myself. *This is a fluke—I'll goof up tomorrow,* I think. So I become nervous, and the first time I fall short of perfection I chide myself.

I can do the opposite. I can encourage myself and cheer myself on. This is not a fake, sugar-coated approach to life. I have a promise from God that he will complete the good work he has begun within me. God is as concerned about my progress as I am, even more. Outward circumstances may worsen, but God's work continues.

So I don't get down if my resolve to eat sensibly gets sloppy or I lose my temper with a difficult person. I start over and go on. I am confident that good things are not in the past, but in the present and the future.

Thank you, God, for believing in me much more than I believe in myself.

REFLECT | *God will continue the good work he has begun in me.*

Day 320 Interested in Others

READ | Philippians 2:4
Each of you should look not only to your own interests, but also to the interests of others.

As I lose my desperate self-absorption, I find that I'm genuinely interested in others and their welfare. As I let go of my self-pity, I feel the pain of others' struggles, and I see them with a more caring perspective. As I learn to feel the feelings I've masked, I'm not so afraid of intimate friendships. And paradoxically, as I share my own neediness, I respect others more because I'm not feeling superior to them for being ones who always give but never receive.

Being interested in others nourishes the spiritual qualities I've prayed for: love, patience, kindness, and gentleness. That's how spiritual growth works. God transforms me when I'm not even aware of it.

God, give me a heart for others, and help me care for
them in healthy ways.

R E F L E C T | *Serenity involves acknowledging the value of
each person.*

√Day 321 Self-Pity

R E A D | Philippians 2:14
Do everything without complaining or arguing.

My self-pity manifests itself in the form of complaining.
I don't like the way I'm treated, I don't like the people in
charge, I don't like the weather. Sometimes I gripe directly
to God: Why is he letting me down? Why can't I have a taste
of success? Why is life so unfair?

Listening to others who also struggle as I do helps me
see that I feel sorry for myself because of my narrow perspective. As I listen objectively to them, I see that I often block
out logic. That person didn't slight me—she just didn't see
me. The people in charge have struggles beyond what I can
imagine. I don't like the rain, but the earth needs it.

When I crawl out of my little world and see people and
situations more objectively, I don't feel sorry for myself.

God, teach me to see life more objectively, not from my
own narrow point of view.

R E F L E C T | *I can crawl outside myself and see life from a
more logical perspective.*

Day 322 Eager to Keep Going

R E A D | Philippians 3:12
Not that I have already obtained all this, or have already been made perfect, but I press on to take hold of that for which Christ Jesus took hold of me.

By rereading my journals or bumping into a long-ago acquaintance, it becomes obvious that I'm becoming a different person.

I get excited about the idea of becoming truly whole from the heart—not even noticing the aroma of a nearby bakery, not flinching in the least when I pass a mirror. Could I ever have the serenity I see in people who have been on this journey for a long time?

So I press on, and on, and on, one day at a time, quietly doing the footwork that needs to be done today. The more I press on, the more I understand myself and the more I see the purposes for which Christ Jesus took hold of me.

God, thank you for how far you've brought me and for how far you're going to take me.

R E F L E C T | *As my obsession slowly fades, I become more excited about what God has in store for me.*

Day 323 Living in the Past

R E A D | Philippians 3:13–14
One thing I do: Forgetting what is behind and straining toward what is ahead, I press on toward the goal to win the prize for which God has called me. . . .

There are many reasons for regret: the people I hurt, the opportunities I missed, the unrepairable abuse I did to my body. If I live in regret, I'll beat myself up, and that pushes me further behind.

I can choose instead to make amends and restitution. I can choose to admit my humanity—yes, I made many, many mistakes. I can choose to discover my character defects and surrender them to God to be turned into strengths.

Even when I consider the most unforgivable things I've done, I remember that today's verse was written by Paul, a former murderer (of the first Christians) turned apostle.

Who am I not to forgive myself when God is so forgiving?

Forgive me, God, for the mistakes of my past and help me use them to live today.

REFLECT | *I can't change my past, but I can move far beyond it.*

Day 324 Back to Basics

READ | Philippians 4:6
Do not be anxious about anything, but in everything, by prayer and petition, with thanksgiving, present your requests to God.

I clench my teeth when someone tosses off the cliché "Just pray about it." It's a cliché in the sense that many people say it, but it's not trite or simple. When I stop to pray about something, it forces me to sort things out in

God's presence, and I often see a new slant on it. I see ways I've been wrong or new possibilities that haven't occurred to me before.

Sometimes I forget to bring the simplest things before God: choosing or refining my eating plan, facing a potluck dinner, eating out with friends. But when I do, God answers in his time. Someone I trust makes a helpful suggestion, or God helps me remember comments people have made. Sometimes I sense that he is slowing me down to get me in sync with his timing.

Lord, make your ways and timing plain to me.

REFLECT | *God is big enough to be concerned about little things.*

Day 325 Negative Thinking

READ | Philippians 4:8
Finally, brothers, whatever is true, whatever is noble, whatever is right, whatever is pure, whatever is lovely, whatever is admirable—if anything is excellent or praiseworthy—think about such things.

I didn't call it distrust, I called it facing reality. I figured that anything that could go wrong would go wrong, but I didn't espouse it as cheerfully as those who quote Murphy's Law do. I had a me-against-the-world attitude, and I figured that if someone could get mad at me they probably would. I lived in fear that my house could burn down or my child could die tomorrow.

Now I see that these crises are possibilities, but I refuse to worry about them. I can assume the best and even be right at times. I enjoy life more because I see the good in others and appreciate it. Someday soon I hope to be one of those interesting people who always find good in unexpected people and places.

God, help me shed my cynical ways and focus on the many positive things you've done on this earth.

REFLECT | *Trusting means choosing to be optimistic until I'm given reasonable evidence to think otherwise.*

Day 326 Overachievers

READ | Philippians 4:13
I can do everything through him who gives me strength.

I used to think this verse meant I could do everything so I should do everything. I accepted positions I didn't like or feel compatible with because I thought God loved super-achievers. Besides, it made me feel so worthwhile to "do it all."

Now I see that doing everything means that I wait for God to define just what *everything* may be. If I don't want to do something, I explain this to God and wait for him to change my mind. If he doesn't, I don't do it. I trust that God will not browbeat me into working at things I hate, but that he will work through me and in me, giving me not only strength, but also appropriate conviction and desire.

Thank you, God, for the strength you provide to help me do everything I should do, today.

REFLECT | *God provides strength for the tasks I need to do.*

Day 327 Giving Back Without Fixing

READ | Colossians 2:2
My purpose is that they may be encouraged in heart and united in love, so that they may have the full riches of complete understanding.

One way to fix people is to help them but limit them in some way by crossing their boundaries. Because I feel grandiose, I think they must follow my advice to live correctly. Because I feel entangled, I feel their failure or success reflects on me. Because I feel controlling, I will be disappointed if they don't copy me or follow my advice.

I'm learning to help others, but to let them make their own choices. They don't have to do things my way. When I function this way as a friend, parent, spouse, mentor, or partner in a project, I feel content. I am fulfilling one of my purposes in life—to assist others in finding maturity and wholeness, knowing that their growth doesn't depend on me but on God and their own choices.

God, teach me to love people and help them
with no strings attached.

REFLECT | *To truly help others is to equip them to help themselves.*

Day 328 My Hiding Place

READ | Colossians 3:3
For you died, and your life is now hidden with Christ in God.

As I gradually surrender more and more of myself to God, my desires become more aligned with his. It feels to me as if our identities have blended, as if there's an indistinct line where I stop and God begins. (This line is probably obvious to God, especially on days when I want to have a candy bar and he would rather I had serenity.)

I used to hide to escape, but this being hidden with Christ is different. Being hidden in God creates a healthy, safe place. Here I talk, trust, and feel without the drivenness. Here I find acceptance and love. I can tell when I have stepped out of my hiding place because the drivenness returns. When I see it happening, I retreat once again.

Thank you, God, for allowing me to hide myself in you.

REFLECT | *I align my thoughts and desires with God's.*

Day 329 Forgiving Those I Fear

READ | Colossians 3:13
Bear with each other and forgive whatever grievances you may have against one another. Forgive as the Lord forgave you.

Forgiveness can be scary. If I release my resentments, I make myself vulnerable to be hurt again. The people I resent probably aren't going to change, so how will I protect myself from them? What will I do when they trample my boundaries again by insulting me, ignoring me, or hurting me?

I ask God to be my protector. When I face the people I fear, I ask God to intervene and remind me of my worth in him, to remind me of the truth about myself if they tell lies about me, and to remind me that he loves me as they are unable to do.

Only when I believe that God is my protector can I forgive.

Please, God, help me forgive those I fear. Stand between them and me as a strong and sturdy guardian angel.

R E F L E C T | *God can provide the protection I need to help me forgive others.*

✓Day 330 Rich Reading

R E A D | Colossians 3:16a
Let the word of Christ dwell in you richly.

My prayer and meditation life can get airy and meaningless when I'm not making concrete contact with God by reading the words he has placed on earth for me. I understand the Bible to be his love letter to me so that I may stand in the confidence that I am loved. It helps me know God's will for me.

Reading Scripture also keeps my relationship with God from becoming one-sided with me talking to him all the time. I want to hear God's input about my life.

I want to read about the struggles of those who have gone before me and how they overcame their personal character defects. I want to see how unlikely people such as Moses (an escaped convict), Rahab (a prostitute), and Matthew (an extortionist) became useful to God. This reassures me that there is hope for me!

God, help me reorganize and be receptive to what you are saying to me through your Word.

R E F L E C T | *I can sense the love of God and know his true character as I read about him in the Bible.*

Day 331 Pleasing God

READ | 1 Thessalonians 2:4
We are not trying to please men but God, who tests our hearts.

What does it take to quit trying to please people so much? This happens only when I find someone more important to please. Surrendering my character defects to God is teaching me to please him first. My conscience nudges me daily, asking, "Who are you trying to please now?" Gradually I change my people-pleasing behaviors until I care less and less about what others think.

Slowly my desires are beginning to coincide with God's enough that I can try to please myself. As I quiet the drivenness inside me, I trust my instincts and intuition, and I feel comfortable with the choices I make.

God, I am grateful that my simple growth pleases you and that you teach me to please the best parts of myself.

REFLECT | *Seeking God's approval first dissolves my people-pleasing ways.*

Day 332 Grateful Anyway

READ | 1 Thessalonians 5:18
Give thanks in all circumstances, for this God's will for you in Christ Jesus.

I'm good at listing for God the things I would like to have that he isn't providing. I see what others around me have or I see what I could have—and I want all of it!

Being thankful for what I have means I trust that God provides exactly what I need. If I needed one more thing, one more friendship, one more success, he would provide it.

If I ask God for something and he doesn't give it to me, I trust he has a good reason. Perhaps there's a wiser path to what I want. After all, when I begged for relief from my destructive eating, he didn't miraculously free me. He put me on a path of growth and struggle. I will emerge a much wiser person for doing it his way.

I thank you, God, for all my circumstances, even the ones that baffle and hurt me. I trust you in these circumstances.

REFLECT | *Gratefulness relieves my inner neediness.*

Day 333 Taking Financial Responsibility

READ | 2 Thessalonians 3:7–8
We were not idle when we were with you, nor did we eat anyone's food without paying for it.

Now that I'm abandoning my magical thinking, I see that most "free" things aren't free. I may get a free dinner for watching a presentation, but I pay the price of resisting the presenter's pressure tactics. Wasn't that part of the deal? Didn't I agree to be pressured (have my boundaries violated!) so I could have a free dinner?

Since my healing and wholeness are rooted in a clear conscience, I can no longer afford to get something for nothing. I can't let the same person take me out to lunch over and over without paying her back in some way. I don't try to get a good deal from a friend; if anything, I want to pay my friend well. I keep relationships from being tainted by taking responsibility for my own finances and resources.

Stop me, God, before I run up debts to people
who love me.

REFLECT | *Paying my way is less expensive in the long run.*

Day 334 Cutting Corners?

READ | 1 Timothy 4:15
Be diligent in these matters; give yourself wholly to them, so that everyone may see your progress.

When I scoop out my portion from the serving dish, how I want to help myself to a more than generous portion! As I finish that first helping, I want to change my eating plan and decide that two helpings are permissible. And when I arrive at a party, I suddenly wish that my personal goals included a handful of M&Ms and roasted almonds just at parties.

Changing my eating plan on the spur of the moment is a subtle way of saying that I don't trust God to provide me with the physical sustenance and emotional support I need. A prayerfully considered eating plan that is not too strict or too lenient can be a powerful tool only if I diligently follow it.

When I allow myself to become sloppy with my commitment to healthy eating, I admit to God that I'm not trusting him, and I ask him to help me trust him more.

God, give me more diligence in following
the abstinence I have chosen.

Day 335 Simply Content

READ | 1 Timothy 6:6–8

But godliness with contentment is great gain. For we brought nothing into this world, and we can take nothing out of it. But if we have food and clothing we will be content with that.

My personal neediness has convinced me to make a big deal out of everything. If I'm shopping, I must buy too much. If I'm looking for a place to live, it must be the best. If I'm eating a meal, it must include all my favorite foods. I used to think this would make me happy.

Godliness with contentment means that I can be happy with a simple lifestyle. I can enjoy simple pleasures such as taking walks with friends, curling up with a book, and playing volleyball. I don't have to outdo anyone or prove anything to anyone.

I know I am loved by God and by many other people. I know that I'm growing. I know that even when I don't know exactly what's going on, I have the tools to survive.

God, place in me a love for simplicity
to fuel my healing.

REFLECT | *When I keep it simple, I can make it.*

Day 336 Malignant Obsession

READ | 1 Timothy 6:10
For the love of money is a root of all kinds of evil.

When my peace and happiness revolve around a thing, it absorbs and betrays me and puts me on the brink of various kinds of evil. When I am obsessed with food and thinness, it becomes poison to me. When I watch too much television, I don't listen to my family and friends. When I am hooked on my career, I confuse making a living with making a life.

I can find balance by copying the attitudes of mature people around me. As I get used to the feeling of balance, I get better at detecting the drivenness when it first appears. Even before I feel the thunder of it, I talk to someone about it. I become accountable for it. I release the thing before it becomes an obsession.

Teach me, God, to sense my drivenness and face it
before it takes over.

REFLECT | *I love people and use things instead of loving things and using people.*

Day 337 Assertiveness

READ | 2 Timothy 1:7
For God did not give us a spirit of timidity, but a spirit of power, of love and of self-discipline.

Stepping back from my old eating patterns and stepping into a new kind of wholeness has helped me stand up for myself more than ever before. Instead of indulging in fear, I ask God for power; instead of indulging in selfishness, I ask God for love; instead of indulging in laziness, I ask God for self-discipline. It was those feelings of fear, selfishness, and laziness that contributed to my need to eat.

As I surrender each of these defects to God, I'm not so needy and I can assert myself more. The love and self-discipline I'm learning help me balance my assertiveness so that I'm neither inappropriately aggressive nor shy and withdrawn.

Life isn't as scary and confusing as it once was.

Thank you, God, for giving me this spirit of power, love, and self-discipline.

REFLECT | *I can not only face food, but I can also assert myself in appropriate ways.*

Day 338 Making Peace

READ | 2 Timothy 2:23
Don't have anything to do with foolish and stupid arguments, because you know they produce quarrels.

267

I argue in many different ways. Sometimes I work so hard to prove my point that I alienate others in the process. At other times, I nitpick because someone is talking about my pet peeve or a celebrity I don't like. At still other times a restless grouchiness creeps up within me. It's like a lion I can't tame, and it makes me itch to start a squabble. I feel as if nothing that anyone does is right.

Now I know that living with a greater peace is an option. I can choose to get away and journal, pray, or talk to someone. I can take a walk or a shower and release it. I can state my position and be done with it. I can agree to disagree and feel at peace, even though everyone doesn't agree with me—even if no one agrees with me.

God, help me choose peace when I feel cantankerous.

REFLECT | *It takes two to quarrel, and I choose not to participate.*

Day 339 Resentments

READ | 2 Timothy 2:24
And the Lord's servant . . . must be kind to everyone, able to teach, not resentful.

My resentments are some of the many precious things I am surrendering to God. Some of them have been with me for years, and I have nursed them and kept them healthy. It's as if they are longtime companions.

But nurturing these resentments chained me to my compulsion. Resenting people and circumstances made me grouchy, gossipy, and negative. These feelings made me want to compulsively eat too much or too little. Because of them, I have hurt people and limited my growth severely.

Listing these resentments is freeing me from bondage. I let go, I make amends, and I feel freed to have a generous attitude toward others.

God, help me to be willing to surrender my known resentments to you.

REFLECT | *Resentments keep me in bondage.*

Day 340 Defensiveness Falls Away

READ | Titus 1:15
To the pure, all things are pure, but to those who are corrupted and do not believe, nothing is pure.

I have been so quick to judge myself without mercy that I tend to think others are judging me, too. I have assumed that others were attacking me, or I've taken comments personally that were not intended to hurt me. At times I have even been a commando in these relationships, making quick, destructive raids against those I perceived as my enemies.

As I recover from my disordered eating, my self-esteem is growing. I feel more loved by God and others. This enables me to accept people's words at face value. I have fewer misunderstandings with people.

I become more positive, too; even intentional insults sometimes go over my head, and I don't rush in to defend myself. This is one more facet of God's peace.

God, help me sense your protection of me so soundly
that I lay down my weapons of defense.

REFLECT | *Purity of thoughts can be my best defense.*

Day 341 People Pushings

READ | Philemon 13, 14
*I would have liked to keep him with me. . . . But I did not want to
do anything without your consent, so that any favor you do will be
spontaneous and not forced.*

Sometimes I want something so badly that I feel like
pushing others so I can have it. I want to change someone's
mind, so I try to persuade them with reason after reason.
I want to be chosen for a certain task, and I launch a self-
promotion campaign. I want a friend to hurry up and get
through the pain of her divorce because it hurts too much
to be with her.

But I have come to believe that pushing violates people's
boundaries. When I try to force and convince, I'm acting as
if God were off somewhere sleeping and not doing his part.
When I push and shove, I'm refusing to respect the other
person. I'm acting as if I know much more than they know,
and they would be much better off if they just listened to
me. That's the same grandiosity that used to fuel my old
eating patterns. It must go.

Help me, God, to respect others enough so I don't
interfere with their choices and decisions.

Day 342 Believing in Others

READ | Philemon 21
Confident of your obedience, I write to you, knowing that you will do even more than I ask.

Being a friend to people who are struggling with eating problems is teaching me the power of having confidence in others. At times I have more confidence in these friends than they have in themselves. I can challenge them, recite their strengths, smile confidently, and say, "I believe that you can do this. You've got a lot going for you, so why don't you give it a try?"

That doesn't mean I'll be disappointed or proven wrong if they fail in some way. I haven't expected that they'll be perfect, only that they would try.

It feels risky to trust others so much, but when I look at the progress God is making with me, nothing seems impossible!

God, help me reflect to others some of the confidence you have in me.

REFLECT | *When confidence is shared, it can be multiplied.*

Day 343 A Down-to-Earth Savior

READ | Hebrews 4:15

For we do not have a high priest who is unable to sympathize with our weaknesses, but we have one who has been tempted in every way, just as we are—yet was without sin.

Jesus Christ knows the drivenness within me and how I battle it. At some point he felt driven toward food, and he felt driven toward appearing attractive to others. He sympathizes with me and does not belittle my struggle. He understands that I can sincerely profess to love him but still love food and thinness.

Since Christ was tempted in every way, he knows temptations I will never know. In that sense, he is more human than I am. He is fully human, but still fully God.

So I can "approach the throne of grace with confidence" (Heb. 4:16). This means I can admit anything to God. I don't need to pray, "God, you've probably never heard this before, but . . ." He's heard it, he's seen it, he (through Christ) was tempted to do the same thing, and he understands me.

Thank you, God, for removing my shame by understanding me, knowing me, and loving me.

REFLECT | *I can come to God with all my neediness and my baggage and say, "This is me. Please love me. Please help me."*

✓Day 344 Suffering is OK

READ | Hebrews 5:8

Although he [Jesus] was a son, he learned obedience from what he suffered, and, once made perfect, he became the source of eternal salvation for all who obey him.

Pretending to be fine, OK, even wonderful, is another cultural and religious practice I am trying to shed. If Jesus suffered, so will I. If he had to learn obedience, so do I.

It is not a sign of weakness or ineptness if I go through crises or if I experience pain. Having a perfect, pain-free existence is not a sign that God is working in my life.

As I cooperate with the suffering and brokenness God allows me to experience, I find empowerment and direction. As I admit my struggles, others open up to me and I see that I can help them better by listening and understanding their struggle than by rattling off formulas and advice. People used to be afraid of that old me that appeared to be so together, but they connect better with the new me who admits brokenness.

Keep me transparent before others, God, and help me shed that mask of looking good.

REFLECT | *When I show myself for the broken person I am, God uses me the most.*

Day 345 Accountable to Witnesses

READ | Hebrews 12:1
Therefore since we are surrounded by such a great cloud of witnesses, let us throw off everything that hinders and the sin that so easily entangles, and let us run with perseverance the race marked out for us.

When my old eating patterns and defects of character have entangled me, I have had only one choice. I have made myself accountable to a group member or wise friend. They are my "great cloud of witnesses." I promise to call one of them when I am tempted to eat candy bars for lunch or put down my co-worker.

There is power in accountability. The power doesn't come from my fearing that if I stray, these witnesses won't love me or will be disappointed in me. The power comes from breaking my isolation and joining a team. As I walk through the day and meet my problems, I have a strong sense that these others are present with me. Because of their strength, I don't become entangled again. Their example, their love for me, their determination fills in where mine falls away.

Thank you, God, for friends I can trust and for how they help me untangle myself.

REFLECT | *Nothing beats teamwork.*

Day 346 Too Dependent on Others

READ | Hebrews 13:5
God has said, "Never will I leave you; never will I forsake you."

Only God can promise never to leave me, although I try to extract this promise from my spouse, relatives, and friends. I don't come out and say this, of course, but I expect these people who love me to never move away, to never be occupied with anyone else, to never miss an intuitive cue that I am lonely and need them.

As I maintain conscious contact with God more often and understand that he is the only one who will never leave me, I can accept the normal distractedness of those I love. I can love these people without making heavy demands on their time or violating their privacy. I can lower my expectations of them and thank them for whatever encouragement and companionship they are able to give.

God, help me not to expect from others the kind of comfort and companionship that comes only from you.

REFLECT | *I can be a better friend when God is my chief friend.*

Day 347 These Truths Were Made for Walking

READ | James 1:22
Do not merely listen to the word, and so deceive yourselves. Do what it says.

Learning the truth about over-eating and dieting isn't enough. Talking to others about my feelings isn't enough. I have to follow through. As I meet each obstacle in life, I can surrender my will. I can confront my negative thoughts with the truth that I am valued and loved by God.

What if I am too rebellious or too lazy to pursue healing today? Should I give up?

No, I can pray to be willing to be willing. I can do everything that I am willing to do. Others may even lose patience with me, but when I ask God to release in me a willingness, I know it will happen.

God, help me to be willing to give up whatever is
blocking my progress.

REFLECT | *I find power as I turn each obstacle over to God.*

Day 348 Being Right Isn't Enough

READ | James 2:13
Mercy triumphs over judgment!

There's more to life than being right. God is the best proof of that. He is perfectly right, but even better, he is perfectly merciful. Even though I deserve judgment, he suspends judgment and lets mercy win.

Can I suspend judgment? Do I have to be right all the time? Can I overlook the faults of others? Can I give others a break?

Being right used to feel so good. Now, showing mercy feels even better. Mercy goes beyond judgment. It fills the gap between the flawed persons that people are and the perfect persons God intends for them to be. I can look at the negative facts in a situation, but temper my conclusions with mercy. I feel closer to my father God when I imitate him this way.

Help me, God, to show mercy to the people I have been
harsh with.

REFLECT | *Love surpasses rightness.*

Day 349 Envy Comes Knocking

READ | James 3:16

For where you have envy and selfish ambition, there you find disor-der and every evil practice.

On some days the grass looks greener everywhere else but in my yard. This person is thinner, that one is more attractive, another one makes more money. When I feel envious, I dislike people I don't even know and wish the worst on people I do know.

To set aside envy, I remember the importance of having character instead of possessions. I look at how far God has brought me. He didn't create me to be all things to all people, but to fulfill the purposes he is revealing to me. I find contentment in continuing to discover those purposes, and I'm learning to enjoy watching others discover theirs.

God, help me focus on what you've given me to do,
and help me to be thankful for the help and
achievements of others.

REFLECT | *When I'm at peace with who I'm becoming, I'm free from envy.*

Day 350 Resisting the Enemy

READ | James 4:7

Submit yourself, then, to God. Resist the devil, and he will flee from you.

My spiritual enemy deceives me with lies. These lies wage war on my mind:

- You will always look stupid.
- You will never get anywhere in life.
- No one really likes you.

I resist this enemy by speaking the truth back and renouncing the lies:

- My body isn't perfect, but God loves me as I am. I am satisfied with the way I look.
- I am cooperating with God to achieve what he wants me to achieve.
- Some people like me, and I'm thankful for that.

I resist this enemy most effectively when I renounce his lies and continue surrendering myself to God.

God, help me recognize the enemy's lies and
speak the truth aloud.

REFLECT | *I am responsible for speaking the truth to counteract the enemy's lies.*

Day 351 Giving Up My Defects of Character

READ | James 4:10
Humble yourselves before the Lord, and he will lift you up.

It's one thing to admit my character defects of self-pity and rage, but it's another to give them to God. To be honest, I've needed them. I've used them to survive. How will I get anyone's attention if I don't feel sorry for myself, fly into a rage, or try to impress them? Will I cease to exist to others?

Sometimes it is hard to be willing to get rid of them. I'll have to let go of all the control, the inner neediness, and the attempts to patch myself up. I can lean on the seemingly ridiculous idea that God will rescue me once I quit rescuing myself.

This doesn't sound like humility, but that's what it is. It's admitting powerlessness. It's admitting that I'm a flawed human being, and that only God is powerful enough to heal me.

God, I admit my powerlessness to you once again and ask you to lift my defects of character from me.

REFLECT | *To admit powerlessness is a step of humility.*

Day 352 Hearing God's Spontaneous Will

READ | James 4:13, 15

Now listen, you who say, "Today or tomorrow we will go to this or that city, spend a year there, carry on business and make money." Instead, you ought to say, "If it is the Lord's will, we will live and do this or that."

I used to be so smart! I had my life planned, my friends' lives planned, and my parents' lives planned. Each vacation was the playing out of a well-rehearsed plot. That control was necessary either to practice my eating problem or to try to stop it. I was spontaneous sometimes—but only to act out my disordered eating. It ruled everything!

As I'm growing less needy I experience the new thrills of a normal, healthy spontaneity. Life is more fun, and I don't feel guilty all the time. As I dismantle my control tower attitude, I hear God speaking to me more clearly. I hear him speaking to me through my friends, my family, and my better impulses. I now have the freedom to follow them.

Help me listen to you, God, instead
of to my own efforts to control.

REFLECT | *I listen to God's will as it is revealed to me.*

Day 353 Coming Clean

READ | James 5:16
Therefore, confess your sins to each other and pray for each other so that you may be healed.

Confessing my faults to others was one of the missing elements of my faith. Now I find cleansing and empowerment in admitting to other human beings the exact nature of my wrongs. I make no excuses, and I present myself in a transparent way: I overate; I am jealous of my friend; I fear the worst in this and every situation.

Instead of embarrassing others, I find this fresh honesty relieves them. Since they know how flawed I am, they feel free to tell me their faults. Our confessions bond us together in a powerful way.

Our mutual honesty also emblazons their struggles on my mind, and I find myself praying for them spontaneously. As part of their team, I ask God to help them in their desire for progress.

God, give me the courage to be honest about
who I am and what I do.

REFLECT | *Confessing and praying with others makes me part of a healing team.*

Day 354 A Clear Conscience Under Slander

READ | 1 Peter 3:16

[Keep] a clear conscience, so that those who speak maliciously against your good behavior in Christ may be ashamed of their slander.

When office gossip spread about me, when someone accused me, and when I was misrepresented, I thought about turning to food. But now that I'm clearing my conscience, I feel less driven when this happens. I don't need to defend myself and prove myself right, because my conscience is clear. I still feel hurt, but I don't feel that old inner craziness.

If the slander continues, I have to work hard to keep my thoughts and behavior clear of resentment. Daily I have to surrender my feelings of revenge and my potential sarcastic defense speeches. At times I call a friend and become accountable. When I manage to keep this clear conscience, I find one more facet of serenity in the midst of my chaotic world.

God, help me keep a clear conscience so I may have peace when others slander me.

REFLECT | *My clear conscience helps my behavior speak on my behalf when others slander me.*

Day 355 Sharing What I Have

READ | 1 Peter 4:11

If anyone speaks, he should do it as one speaking the very words of God. If anyone serves, he should do it with the strength God provides, so that in all things God may be praised through Jesus Christ.

As I heal from the inside out, I can cancel any hidden agenda in my speech or service. I serve as God leads me, not to impress, control, or manipulate.

I can't give a sales speech to those who ask me questions about overcoming eating problems, either. I share my strength, hope, and experience, and then I shut my mouth. I listen carefully, showing inquirers the love and respect they may not have shown themselves in years.

And when pastors, therapists, or doctors quiz me, I boldly share my experience with these experts, too. I'm careful to listen to my motives and try to get a sense of what God is or is not leading me to say. I don't have to dazzle anyone; I can be myself.

God, lead me to do and say what is your
will for me today.

REFLECT | *I can't change anyone's thinking, but I can pass along the love that I have received.*

√Day 356 Doubting My Progress

READ | 1 Peter 5:8
Be self-controlled and alert. Your enemy the devil prowls around like a roaring lion looking for someone to devour.

When I blow it by eating outside my abstinence, panicking about the future, or becoming upset about small things, I doubt that I've changed at all. I berate myself by asking myself if I should be doing better. I ask myself if I am really making any progress.

It's one thing to be on a path to wholeness and quite another thing to believe it. My spiritual enemy tries to convince me that I am hopeless: I'll never become completely faithful to my desires to eat sensibly; I'll never feel comfortable in life.

I can read my journals and talk to friends I've known for years to reaffirm that yes, I've changed. I rehearse the fact that healing and wholeness is a process, and I'm still growing.

God, help me walk in the truth that I am progressing
on your path for me.

REFLECT | *I can quiet the old, negative thinking that wants to erase the progress I've made.*

Day 357 How Am I Progressing?

READ | 2 Peter 1:5–8

Make every effort to add to your faith goodness; and to goodness, knowledge . . . self-control . . . perseverance . . . godliness . . . brotherly kindness . . . love. For if you possess these qualities in increasing measure, they will keep you from being ineffective and unproductive.

How do I evaluate my progress? Are comparisons unhealthy? Most of them are, but I can compare myself now with:

- what I used to be like. Are my eating habits and character strengths growing and changing even in small ways? Do I find it slightly easier to do the right thing, love others, and stick it out in tough situations?

- what I could be like now without this healing process. If my eating problems had continued to progress unchecked, would I be miserable, much more over weight, or even dead?
- what Christ is like. What Christlike qualities do I need to possess? How am I possessing them in increasing measure?

Progress in these areas indicates that God's work in me is moving along.

Thank you, God, for the work you do within me.

REFLECT | *I evaluate my healing by the progress I'm making.*

Day 358 God, the Rescuer

READ | 2 Peter 2:9
The Lord knows how to rescue godly men from trials.

God rescues me from the clutches of midnight pizza runs, slippery situations, and intimidating people. As I take a daily inventory every night, I can say, "Can you believe I left the drugstore without an ice cream cone? Was that really me?"

Recalling God's excellent track record of rescues gives me courage for the future and helps me depend on him even more. When I find myself overwhelmed at a party full of sweets or an all-you-can-eat salad bar, I can know that God is one step ahead of me. I don't tempt him to rescue me, but I know that if I really need it, he will intervene in some way. Then it's my turn to choose to accept his intervention.

Help me, God, to recall those moments in which you
have rescued me.

REFLECT | *God proves to me every day that he can restore
me to sanity.*

Day 359 Denial

READ | 1 John 1:8
*If we claim to be without sin, we deceive ourselves and the truth is
not in us.*

Denying I have a problem used to feed my eating
struggles and make them grow larger. I'm still tempted to
say, "But it's not unusual to eat that way!"

Even though I admit my powerlessness and surrender it
to God, there are other things I can be in denial about. To
whom do I really need to make amends? What unhealthy
habits am I still holding onto? Am I still behaving compulsively about certain aspects of eating, even though I am
more disciplined in other ways?

My denial shows in different ways. I refuse to consider a
criticism. I push away the thought of becoming accountable
for an unhealthy habit. I make excuses for spending too
much or working too hard when it's really my neediness
driving me.

I know the relief that comes from turning these things
over to God, so I begin by talking these things over with
him.

God, please show me my blind spots.

REFLECT | *It's when I think I've arrived that I'm in trouble.*

Day 360 Never-Ending Forgiveness

READ | 1 John 1:9
If we confess our sins, he is faithful and just and will forgive us our sins and purify us from all unrighteousness.

God promises to forgive my sins no matter what. He doesn't say, "Wait a minute. You have three sins too many this month. Go to the back of the line." He is willing, waiting, and watching for me to come to him and confess my sins so he can forgive me.

This simple access to God and his ready forgiveness make it a little easier for me to make a habit of confessing wrongs as soon as they occur. Sometimes I wait until the end of the day or longer, but I like to turn around immediately and say, "Did you see what I just did, God?" Then I ask his forgiveness, I ask the other person's forgiveness, and I correct the situation.

As confessing to God becomes an immediate habit, I become free to change my behaviors. I'm so glad. It's about time.

God, thank you that you so generously forgive when I ask.

REFLECT | *Some things are better left said.*

Day 361 God's Love

READ | 1 John 3:1
How great is the love the Father has lavished on us, that we should be called children of God!

I keep forgetting that God loves me with a determined and relentless love. God resembles parents who watch with delight as their baby attempts to scoot and roll toward them. They smile and pick up the baby and feed their little one. God doesn't wait for me to do something spectacular before he picks me up. It's enough that I just exist.

This love is not stingy. He lavishes it on me and lets me know that there's more where that came from.

And God's love gives me value; I am worth a great deal in his eyes. His love gives me strength; he will sustain me even though it looks as if everything's against me. His love gives me hope; he will help me find a way to accomplish what needs to be done.

God, don't let me lose sight of your great love for me.

REFLECT | *God is making me a complete person by loving me.*

Day 362 Demanding Love—My Way

READ | 1 John 4:8–9
God is love. This is how God showed his love among us: He sent his one and only Son into the world that we might live through him.

I have mistakenly assumed that God didn't love me because he didn't do everything I asked him to do—especially giving me a smooth, easy life and a perfect, attractive body. I see now that God's love goes much deeper. He does what is best for me no matter how much it costs him.

I make the same mistake with other people—I assume they don't love me unless they do everything I ask them to do. I'm learning to let people show their love in their own way. If I really love them, I won't try to control them by telling them exactly how to prove their love or loyalty to me. I will let them decide that and accept it graciously.

Like God, they may come up with ways that are much better than I would have prescribed. That can be delightful!

Help me, God, to accept other people's love graciously, just as you're teaching me to do with you.

R E F L E C T | *Demanding that love comes to me only in certain forms robs me and others of the joy of love.*

Day 363 Fears and Realities

R E A D | 1 John 4:18
There is no fear in love. But perfect love drives out fear, because fear has to do with punishment. The one who fears is not made perfect in love.

I fear most things. I fear failure and success. I fear rejection and intimacy. I fear looking unattractive and looking attractive. I fear that others are looking at me, and I fear they aren't looking at me. I fear that I disappoint authority figures, and I fear disappointing those who view me as an authority figure.

I'm learning to accept these realities:

- Failures, successes, and disappointments happen to everyone. They are not punishments; they are part of reality. They happen whether or not I fear them.
- God will not forsake me. He will stand by me as I walk through each struggle.

The more I surrender my fears, the less real they become.

God, help me feel confident in your powerful love.

REFLECT | *I have not been condemned to live my life in fear.*

Day 364 Fear of Intimacy

READ | 2 John 12
I hope to visit you and talk with you face to face, so that our joy may be complete.

Receiving a letter as bold and loving as this one from the apostle John would make me wish for an airline strike to keep him away. Could I stand being with someone who liked me that much?

Even though I'm beginning to understand that God values me, I still fear intimacy with others. I'm afraid that if wise, discerning people get close to me, they'll discover that I'm an uneasy, frightened person. Certainly they'll reject me! What if we eat together—will they watch how I eat?

But living one day at a time, I can concern myself only with whom I face today and absorbing the love and intimacy they may offer (if any). I can focus on what it means to give to another person and stop worrying about how well I'm being perceived. I can stop analyzing their behavior and start being myself.

Thank you, God, that people care about me enough that I find intimacy scary. Help me to relax.

REFLECT | *To be loved is to be vulnerable—I'm getting used to that.*

Day 365 Yes, I Am Thirsty

READ | Revelation 22:17
The Spirit and the bride say, "Come!" And let him who hears say, "Come!" Whoever is thirsty, let him come; and whoever wishes, let him take the free gift of the water of life.

I keep thinking that God wants me to be good enough before he can do anything with me. When I'm good, he'll help me. When I'm perfect, he'll like me.

I'm learning that I don't have to be good enough. All I have to do is be willing. When he says, "Come!" I say, "Yes." No matter how many times I fall, I can get back up again.

I can make my neediness work for me instead of against me. My neediness says that I am "whoever is thirsty," and "whoever wishes." With all my brokenness in front of me, I am a prime candidate to be one who surrenders myself and says, "Yes, I will come!"

I shed my shame and I come to you.

REFLECT | *When I surrender, I'm doing what God wants.*

Specific Words Relating to Healing and Wholeness

Abstinence—A more normal eating plan of my own choosing, often three simple meals a day.

Accountability—Making a commitment to try to practice a healthy behavior or abstain from a compulsive one, such as overeating or throwing up.

Amends—Doing what is needed to repair insults or injuries, such as improving my attitudes, correcting my errors, or making financial restitution.

Boundaries—limits or choices I make about time, privacy, familiarity, talents, or anything that defines who I am. I set up healthy boundaries about what I say, what I do, and how closely I identify myself with others. If I don't respect these things in others, I "cross" their boundaries.

Confidentiality—Not revealing to anyone what is shared in weekly meetings or in private conversations with friends, especially those who struggle with eating. It also includes maintaining the anonymity of other persons by not mentioning their involvement in a group.

Conscious Contact with God—Communicating with God throughout the day.

Cycle of Compulsive Behavior—
- preoccupation (thinking about compulsive eating, dieting, purging, or starving)
- ritualization (behavioral patterns I routinely use to try not to behave compulsively)

- compulsive behavior (various forms of severe dieting, overeating, purging, or starving)
- despair (feeling shame and hopelessness for repeating the pattern)

Defects of Character—Flaws that cause me to feel needy, such as self-pity, resentment, laziness, hostility, or fear of rejection.

Denial—Refusing to see my faulty attitudes and behaviors, including not admitting that I have an eating problem or that I'm angry or upset.

God's Grace—God's generous willingness to give me what I need, not what I deserve. Also, God's willingness to empower me to do things that are clearly beyond my ability.

Group Meetings—Safe places in which honest feelings can be shared without threat of rejection; these include Twelve-Step meetings such as Overeaters Anonymous, as well as the weekly meetings that have been central to the 3D Plan since it began.

Inventory—A process of examining my past and present to discover the history and patterns of my eating struggles and my defects of character. This is often done thoroughly in written form one or more times and then informally at the close of each day.

Journaling—Writing my thoughts and feelings as honestly as possible.

Justified—When God removes my blame and guilt and declares me right in his eyes.

Mentor—A partner who has more experience than I do and who can support me and warn me if I'm getting off track;

someone to whom I can be accountable and know that I will be accepted.

No-Crosstalk Rule—A common method of Twelve-Step groups and some other support groups in which I may not interrupt others when they are sharing, even to ask questions or offer comfort.

Spiritual Director—A person trained to have conversations with people to help them discern the presence of God and live out God's call within the context of biblical truth and the Christian community.

Tools—Methods and sources for help on my path to wholeness such as reading books of spiritual encouragement, prayer, Scripture reading, meditation, journaling, practicing various kinds of abstinence, attending weekly meetings, working with a mentor or spiritual director, and writing an inventory.

About Paraclete Press

Who We Are

Paraclete Press is a publisher of books, recordings, and DVDs on Christian spirituality. Our publishing represents a full expression of Christian belief and practice—from Catholic to Evangelical, from Protestant to Orthodox.

We are the publishing arm of the Community of Jesus, an ecumenical monastic community in the Benedictine tradition. As such, we are uniquely positioned in the marketplace without connection to a large corporation and with informal relationships to many branches and denominations of faith.

What We Are Doing

BOOKS | Paraclete publishes books that show the richness and depth of what it means to be Christian. Although Benedictine spirituality is at the heart of all that we do, we publish books that reflect the Christian experience across many cultures, time periods, and houses of worship. We publish books that nourish the vibrant life of the church and its people—books about spiritual practice, formation, history, ideas, and customs.

We have several different series, including the best-selling Living Library, Paraclete Essentials, and Paraclete Giants series of classic texts in contemporary English; A Voice from the Monastery—men and women monastics writing about living a spiritual life today; award-winning literary faith fiction and poetry; and the Active Prayer Series that brings creativity and liveliness to any life of prayer.

RECORDINGS | From Gregorian chant to contemporary American choral works, our music recordings celebrate sacred choral music through the centuries. Paraclete distributes the recordings of the internationally acclaimed choir Gloriæ Dei Cantores, praised for their "rapt and fathomless spiritual intensity" by *American Record Guide*, and the Gloriæ Dei Cantores Schola, which specializes in the study and performance of Gregorian chant. Paraclete is also the exclusive North American distributor of the recordings of the Monastic Choir of St. Peter's Abbey in Solesmes, France, long considered to be a leading authority on Gregorian chant.

DVDS | Our DVDs offer spiritual help, healing, and biblical guidance for life issues: grief and loss, marriage, forgiveness, anger management, facing death, and spiritual formation.

LEARN MORE ABOUT US AT OUR WEB SITE: www.paracletepress.com, or call us toll-free at 1-800-451-5006.

You May Also Be Interested In . . .

Open Your Heart
12 Weeks of Daily Devotions

If you are on a journey of reclaiming your life for God, you may need this wisdom. Walk with Martin Shannon, together with Carol Showalter, and find hope as you consider these topics:

- Learning to Forgive Yourself
- The Need to Be Loved
- Self-righteousness
- Dealing with Feelings of Anger
- Playing God
- How to Make Every Day a New Beginning

$16.95

Echoes of Eternity
Summer Devotions

The oldest Christian traditions invite us to listen when we pray, but the quiet voice of God often seems drowned out by the cares and concerns of the day. This little book offers three months of Scriptural meditations, encouraging you with words of God's love, lasting peace, refreshment and renewal, and daily grace.

$8.95

For the complete line of Your Whole Life resources, visit www.3DYourWholeLife.com or call 1-800-451-5006

THE 3D PLAN
EAT RIGHT · LIVE WELL · LOVE GOD